DEVON AT THE CINEMA

Courtesy Dudley Stidson

The Barn Cinema: Hope Cove 1938.

by

Gordon Chapman

DEVON BOOKS

First Published in Great Britain in 2000 by Devon Books

British Library Cataloguing in Publication Data

Data for this publication is available from the British Library

ISBN 1 85522 758 4

DEVON BOOKS
Official Publisher to Devon County Council

Halsgrove House
Lower Moor Way
Tiverton
Devon EX16 6SS
Tel: 01884 243242
Fax 01884 243325
www.halsgrove.com

Printed and bound in Great Britain by Bookcraft Ltd, Midsomer Norton

DEVON AT THE CINEMA

Dedicated to
Trudi, Simon & Fiona
Movie Buffs All.

"Do come to the Cinema again"

The First Generation of Movie Buffs

*Card, sent on 12th of December 1912,
by the author's Father to his Mother*

Typical Small Town Cinema c1935

FAÇADE

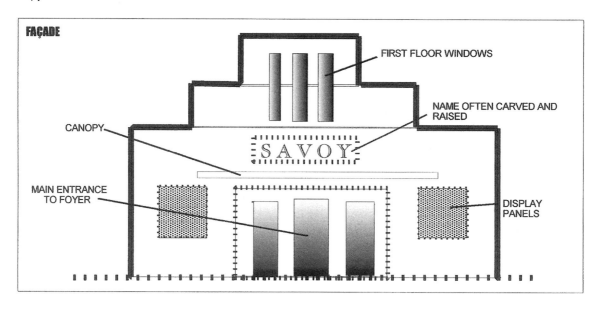

FIRST FLOOR WINDOWS

NAME OFTEN CARVED AND RAISED

CANOPY

SAVOY

MAIN ENTRANCE TO FOYER

DISPLAY PANELS

SIDE ELEVATION

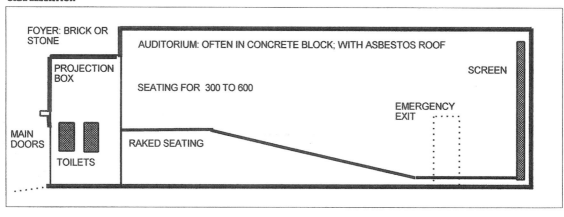

FOYER: BRICK OR STONE

AUDITORIUM: OFTEN IN CONCRETE BLOCK; WITH ASBESTOS ROOF

PROJECTION BOX

SCREEN

SEATING FOR 300 TO 600

EMERGENCY EXIT

MAIN DOORS

RAKED SEATING

TOILETS

PLAN

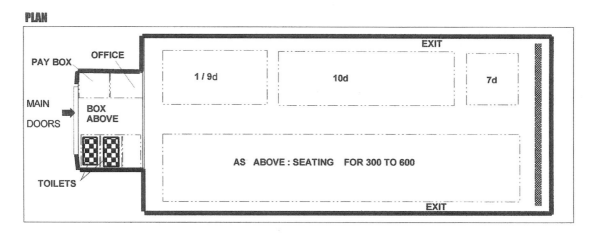

EXIT

PAY BOX

OFFICE

MAIN

DOORS

BOX ABOVE

1 / 9d

10d

7d

AS ABOVE : SEATING FOR 300 TO 600

TOILETS

EXIT

G.C. 2000

Typical Large Town Cinema c1935

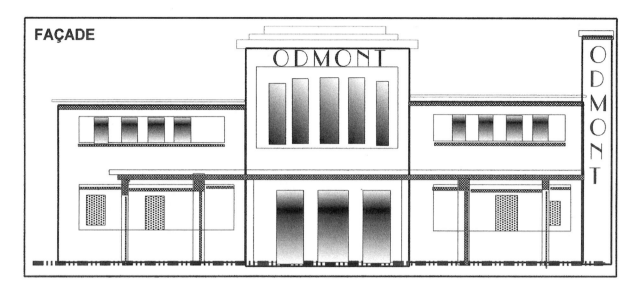

FAÇADE

ODMONT

ODMONT

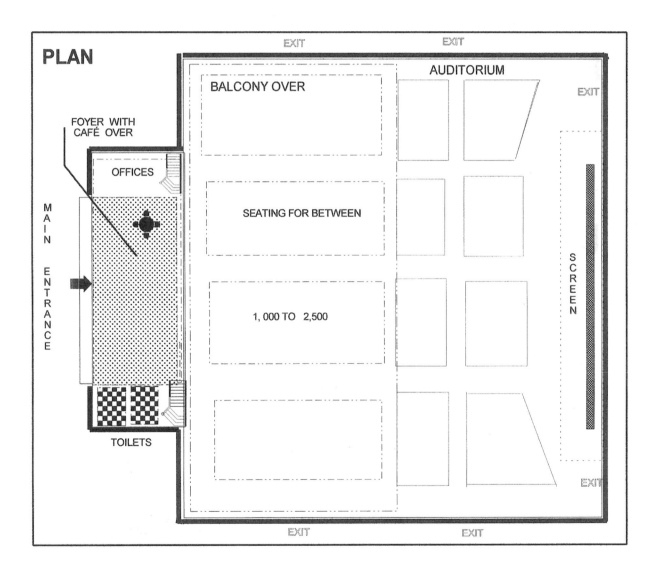

PLAN

EXIT EXIT

AUDITORIUM

EXIT

BALCONY OVER

FOYER WITH
CAFÉ OVER

OFFICES

M
A
I
N

E
N
T
R
A
N
C
E

MAIN ENTRANCE

SEATING FOR BETWEEN

S
C
R
E
E
N

1, 000 TO 2,500

TOILETS

EXIT

EXIT EXIT

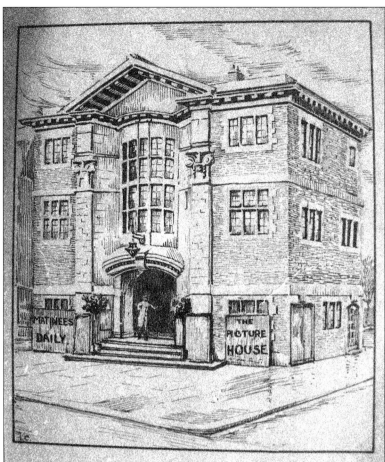

Torbay Cinema, Paignton - Flyer 1913

The Riviera, Teignmouth 1997

DEVON AT THE CINEMA
THE FIRST HUNDRED YEARS

My purpose in undertaking the research on which this book is based was to locate, through visits and written material, and where possible, photographs, any building used for the showing of moving films on a regular, though not necessarily daily basis. It was not intended, at least at that stage, to do an in-depth study of any of these cinemas. It was hoped that when published, this outline research would give to later researchers a basic framework on which to build more detailed studies. Alongside the photographs taken as part of the project, it has been possible to build up a small collection of earlier photographs and other cinema memorabilia. These have been especially valuable where the building no longer exists.

However, as the project advanced, it became clear that some cinemas deserved further study. The first of these is the Torbay Cinema, Paignton, then claimed to be 'the oldest working cinema in Europe'. The Torbay Cinema story is in itself fascinating but what makes it more interesting is its wealth of documentation, both written and pictorial. The decision to do more than just record its position and external features was made the more urgent as for much of the period of the research project the cinema was under threat of closure. In fact, it finally closed on Saturday September 25th 1999. The second cinema to be considered in this way is the Riviera Cinema, Teignmouth whose history tells the whole story of cinema building and conversion in microcosm. In the case of the Torbay Cinema I am greatly indebted to the former manager, Mr J.J. Mann, for unfailing help and encouragement over the whole period of my research. I am equally indebted to the owner of the Riviera Cinema, Mr Peter Prince, whose father purchased the cinema in 1923. Mr Peter Prince has most generously allowed me to quote at length from his own researches into the history of this fascinating building. This cinema also closed early in this new century, in March 2000. As more information came to hand during the period of the research, other cinemas lent themselves to a more detailed examination, making it possible to gain a clearer insight into the history of cinema in Devon over the past hundred years.

Symbols used throughout:

BDC - Bill Douglas Centre
BE - Building extant
Bz - Blitz
CTA - Cinema Theatre Association
CVA - Cinema Veterans Association
CWC - Current Working Cinema
D - Demolished
F - Fire
FE - Façade only extant
FTVYB - British Film & TV Year Book

KD - Kelly's Directory of Devon
KYB - Kine Year Book
MCS - Mercia Cinema Society
PT - Part-time Cinema;
c1912 - Actual date uncertain
[?] Outcome unknown.
The date given in square brackets [ ] after each entry refers to the author's first visit to the cinema / site [ ]S

Author's collection

Kelly's and the Kine Year Book, both invaluable aids to research of this nature.

All quotations taken from interviews were taped by the author on the date given and are held on file, both tape and transcript. [T...]

An Introduction

'.. Thirty years ago it was croquet, fifteen years ago it was cycling, ten years ago it was roller-skating....'

The Times: 9th April 1913   (On the new craze of cinema)

'The most imaginative type of inter-war building was the cinema. Behind the fantasy foyers of Odeons and Gaumonts were the Art-Deco auditoria, where people made their periodic escape into Hollywood.'

The Making of the English Town: David W. Lloyd: Gollancz 1984.

Picture Palaces: Odeon interiors of the 1930s. Taken from the Opening Programme of the Exeter Odeon, 1937.

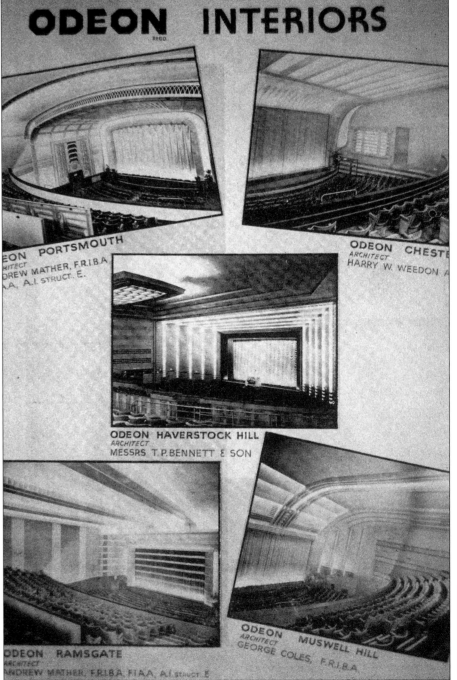

In trying to research the history of cinema buildings in Devon, or indeed anywhere else in the world, one is faced with many difficulties. These may be summarized as follows:-

1. Lack of written and / or photographic evidence.

2. Non-permanent venues.	Fairs, Open Air Cinema	e.g.	Okehampton
3. Change of use.	The Cinema	e.g	Honiton
4. Rebuilding.	The Regent	e.g.	Kingsbridge
5. Multi-Use.	Seven Stars	e.g.	Totnes
6. Demolition.	ABC	e.g.	Exeter
7. Bombing.	Plaza etc.	e.g.	Exeter & Plymouth

Rowlands "Living Pictures" - Seaton 1904

The major problem is that, until recently, no one thought of the Picture Palaces as being worth recording. David W. Lloyd's *The Making of the English Town* is typical here for, despite the quotation given above, there is no other mention of cinema in the whole book. As films were considered ephemeral, so were the places in which they were shown. Another major problem is that, for at least two decades after films began to be shown publicly, they were not necessarily screened in purpose-built cinemas. Anyone with a room long enough and a desire to 'make a quick buck' could and did show films. Finally, as most cinemas were in town centres, they were vulnerable to both bombs and city planners. Given that they were often to be found, at a later date, on prime sites, it is debatable which of the above caused the greatest losses.

Blitz damage in Exeter: the end of several movie houses, such as the Lounge and Palladium.

Demolition of the Exeter ABC 1987

The site of the Picture Palace at Buckfastleigh 1998

In the search for evidence at street level there are many pitfalls. Not the least of these being the fact, as stated above, that many of the buildings used for the showing of films, especially in the early days, were not purpose-built. Exeter is a prime example of this particular problem. Of the twelve buildings so far identified as cinemas in the city, only three, until the coming of the new Picture House in Bartholomew Street, were purpose-built. Examples of this trend can also be found in the Cinema at Honiton, The Bijou in Bideford and the Cosy

Cinema in Topsham. Town halls and other community buildings were often used as part-time cinemas, for example in Bovey Tracey and Budleigh Salterton. These buildings rarely show any outward signs of their use as cinemas. Sometimes, as in the case of the Matthews Hall, Topsham, a chance to view the interior will show the projector ports still in place.

The only evidence to hand on Open-air Cinema in Devon comes from a single poster held in The Museum of Dartmoor Life at Okehampton; even the date is uncertain as no year is given on the poster, only day and month. However, after checking the film *Nero*, which is advertised on the poster, with the BFI , a likely date is 1911. The only other evidence I have found of open-air cinema in this country comes from Hull, where an open-air cinema opened in July 1912, closed for the winter and never re-opened, which was not really surprising given the English climate.

Demolition and bombing leave no traces at all. Who, walking past Boots in Exeter or Littlewoods in Plymouth, would ever guess that here once stood large and imposing picture palaces, in the former case the ABC and in the latter the Regent /Odeon cinema. These are both cases where cinemas have been demolished in the post-war period. The old Fore Street in Devonport once held a number of cinemas: all that is left is the Forum, now a bingo hall, the rest were reduced to rubble in the blitz of 1941.

The outline story of Devon's cinemas is, perhaps, best understood by using the various year maps showing the spread of cinemas over the century since moving pictures began. It should be noted that these maps are based on information taken only from the Kine Year Book. Though this may lead to some slight inaccuracies, it gives the information shown on the maps a common source.

Nero Poster: Okehampton

Site of the Regent/ Odeon, Plymouth

DEVON CINEMAS

1914

✳ Cinema

Ilfracombe ✳
Lynton
Braunton ✳
Appledore
Barnstaple
Bideford ✳
Gt. Torrington
South Molton
Holsworthy
Tiverton ✳
Okehampton
Cullompton
Crediton
Chagford
Honiton
Moreton'h
✳ ✳ ✳ ✳ ✳ ✳
Tavistock
EXETER ✳ ✳ ✳ ✳ ✳   Ottery St. Mary
Bovey
Topsham
Axminster
Princetown
Sidmouth
Ashburton
Seaton
Buckfastleigh
Budleigh
Exmouth ✳
✳ ✳ ✳ ✳ ✳
Newton Abbot
Dawlish
Devonport ✳ ✳ ✳ ✳ ✳
✳ ✳
Teignmouth ✳
Plympton
Plymouth   Ivybridge
✳ ✳ ✳ ✳ ✳ ✳
Totnes ✳
Torquay ✳ ✳ ✳
Paignton ✳
Brixham ✳
Kingsbridge
Dartmouth ✳ ✳
Salcombe

N.B. These figures are taken from KYB 1914

Gordon Chapman: January 1999

By 1914 Devon had, taking the figures from the Kine Year Book, 43 cinemas in 15 towns, though Kelly's Directory for the same year gives 31 cinemas in 17 towns. This pattern of distribution, heavily weighted to the south of the county, was to remain constant, and it is still true today. To some extent this reflected both the normal distribution of population and the pattern of tourism which had grown up and developed in the nineteenth century. The cinemas marked will only be those with fixed venues, though not all will be purpose-built cinemas. Not shown will be the very early and popular fairground and travelling 'one night stands'. For many people these tent shows were their first introduction to the magic of the movies.

DEVON CINEMAS
1895 - 1914

Important films in circulation by 1914.

The Great Train Robbery	1903 - US - Edwin S Porter	(Ran for 12 minutes)
Rescued by Rover	1905 - UK - C. Hepworth	(Cost £8 . 7. 6d)
Ben Hur	1908 - US - S. Olcott	(The first of 3 versions to date)
Delhi Durbar	1910 - UK - Urban	(Kinemacolour)
Queen Elizabeth	1912 - FR -	(Starring Sarah Bernhardt)
Quo Vadis	1912 - IT -	(Ran for 2 hours)

Quo Vadis 1912, one of the very first epics. An Italian film that influenced D.W. Griffith.

Map 1: Devon Cinemas 1895 - 1914

As can be seen by even a brief study of the map, there was a concentration of cinemas in the south of the county. The pattern was to remain constant throughout the whole period under review. This pattern reflects both the geography of the county and, to some extent, the pattern of tourism, which began in the nineteenth century. At this stage, as might be expected, Plymouth led the field, with Exeter and Devonport following. Of the rest, only Ilfracombe had more than one cinema. This gives a total of 31 cinemas in 17 towns.

Barnstaple Fair 1907, "Living Pictures". Often the first movies seen in Devon, especially in rural areas.

The Regent, Axminster 1998

The Regent, Axminster [detail]

Chaplin in The Kid *(1921) with Jackie Coogan*

AXMINSTER CINEMAS

Cinema Picture Palace / Regent: Castle Hill: c1914 - c1930   BE

This cinema, which was better known as the Regent Cinema, opened prior to the Great War, and continued into the 1920s. When a second cinema was opened in the town, the Regent was forced to close. The building, or at least part of the façade, is still extant but the interior is much changed. When I visited the site in June 1998, there was no doubt that this had once been a cinema, with the name boldly standing out from the façade. The Regent was sited in the old open market at the top of Castle Hill. In a letter I received in 1996 I was given the following delightful and informative description of the cinema in 1920:

'I remember going to my first visit to the cinema at the age of 5, that was in 1920, at the Regent in Market Square. I was taken there by my uncle, the film was Charlie Chaplin and Jackie Coogan in The Kid. *That was of course in the days of the old silent films. It was always accompanied by a piano player, who was a Mrs Wench, who lived in a cottage at Penny's Terrace. Saturday afternoons was always a matinée for the children, admission 2d. There was always a mad rush to get a seat in the front row. The cinema was run by a Mr Walford, who had a wooden leg. There was a ladder to get up to the projection box, how he got up there I don't know, but he did. Once a year it was taken over by [a] travelling company which put on shows for that week. .....the leading light was a gentleman named Alf Beverlee... Then came the 'Talkies' , the first one at the Regent was The White Hell of Pitz Palu which was a mountain drama.'* [5.6.98]

It may be worth noting at this point that 'mountain dramas' were a very popular genre in the German cinema at this period.

BARNSTAPLE CINEMAS

Picture Palace   2 Silver Street   c1914 - ??   [?]

This is another cinema that opened prior to the Great War. By 1919 the proprietor was Mr Wilfred E. Jones. It appears that, for a while, it was known as the Cosy Cinema. When I visited Barnstaple in 1997, I could find no trace of this cinema although it appears in Kelly's Directory (hereafter referred to as KD) as late as 1923.

Bideford Cinemas:

Bijou   **Lower Gunstone**   **c 1914 - ??**   **BE**

Before going on to speak of Bideford's cinemas, I must make acknowledgement of the help given to me by Mr Peter Christie, who gave up an afternoon to take me on a guided tour of the town and point out the sites of all the town's cinemas.

The Bijou was situated in Lower Gunstone and when I visited the town (July 1997) the building was still extant. It is in fact the upper portion of the building and I assumed that it must have been quite a small cinema. However, when checking in the 1917 KYB, I find the seating given as 400. It opened sometime prior to 1914, when it appears in KD but is not shown in the 1919 directory. It would seem to be one of those short-lived cinemas that cashed in on the cinema craze of the pre-war years, but was unable, for reasons unknown, to continue in business. [16.7.97]

The Bijou, Bideford.

The Bijou & Palladium, Bideford

Electric Palace   **c1914 - ?**   **[?]**

The Electric Palace, Bideford, appears in the 1914 edition of the Kinematograph Year Book (hereafter referred to as KYB), but I have no other information on this cinema. It could be that it later became the Palladium cinema, but this is pure guess work. Unfortunately the KYB gives only the name, with no address or other information that might help to establish its history.

Brixham Cinemas.

1. The Electric Theatre   **c1914 - 1966**   **BE**

This is another cinema that appears in the KYB but does not feature in KD of 1914. However, here we have at least the owner, given as A.O. Ellis, and the seating as 500. The Ellis family will feature often in the following pages. This is the first time they appear and they were obviously among the first in Devon to set about creating a circuit of cinemas. At this date A.O. Ellis was also managing the Northfield Picture Palace in Ilfracombe, and A.W. Ellis was owner of the Cinema Picture Palace in Sidmouth. More of this cinema later.

The Electric Theatre, Brixham. Still drawing crowds, but without that sense of fun.

Budleigh Salterton Cinemas

Masonic Hall   **West Hill**   **1912 - 1918**   **[?]**

The Masonic Hall on West Hill was the earliest venue for films in Budleigh. However, there were to be at least two more homes for the 'flicks' in this small town: the building housing the last of these three venues is still extant and was last used, on a 'one night stand' basis, for the showing of films in February 1997. This show, which my wife and I attended, included Porter's 1903 *The Great Train Robbery*, along with a selection of early work by the Walt Disney Studio.

Palladium, Dartmouth.
Still recognisable to former fans.

Author's Collection

Dartmouth Cinemas

Palladium Electric Theatre: **Hanover Street**   **c1914 - c1918**   **BE**

I had been unable to find any details of this cinema beyond the fact that it appeared in KD for 1914 and had gone by 1919, and I thought that it may well have been one of the several cinemas that failed to survive the Great War. The reasons behind these war-time failures will be discussed in the next section. However, when I came to look more closely at street names in Dartmouth, a solution presented itself. There was a Cinedrome in Anzac Street by 1919. This looked like a case of the street changing its name, for obvious reasons at this time, and a telephone call to the Dartmouth Museum confirmed this. I am told that nearby are dwellings still known as Hanover Cottages. In fact there was a cinema on this site until after the Second World War. It is now a small shopping arcade, but the name 'Palladium' can still be seen above the Anzac Street entrance. [7.5.98]

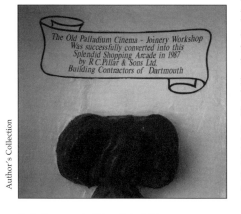

Palladium, part of the original décor
one assumes.

Roseville Electric Theatre   **Victoria Road** **c1914 - c1920s**   **D**

As with the Palladium in Hanover Street, so with the Roseville Electric Theatre in Victoria Road - little seems to be known. It was open by 1914 but had disappeared from the directories by 1923. The proprietor in 1914 was William George Hilt. One suspects that it was a small, family-run cinema which was unable to meet the challenge for patrons as other, and possibly more palatial, picture palaces opened in the town. This is only supposition but fits the pattern for the period. I understand that a skating rink and tennis courts replaced the cinema.

Dawlish Cinemas

Walfords C.E.V. **Chapel Street** **c1911 - ??** **[?]**

Apart from the name, address and that it was open by 1914, I have been unable to trace any other information on this early cinema. Mr Clarence Walford was at this time running Walford's Cinema Palace in Tavistock, and it seems almost certain that this was another of his enterprises. Indeed, even by this early date certain names begin to appear, names that were to play an important role in the history of cinema in Devon. Besides Mr Walford, we find the following names at this time: Mr William Linsdell running two cinemas in Plymouth, the Ellis family running cinemas as far apart as Sidmouth and Ilfracombe, and Mr Albany Ward who over the years was to build up a circuit of cinemas. Mr C. Scott was to repeat this pattern again after the Second World War. He in his turn has been followed by Mr Peter Hoare, who runs six cinemas at the present time, four of them in Devon. As Mr Hoare remarked when I spoke to him in 1997, Devon is a rural county and therefore, although it had few Picture Palaces in the real sense of that term, it did have a large number of small to medium-sized picture houses. It is this type of hall that makes possible the involvement of the local entrepreneur in the cinema business. This it has done from the start of the century to the present; with the advent of the multiplex one wonders how long this 'local involvement' can last. When I spoke to Mr. Pope, who owns and runs the Carlton Cinema in Okehampton, he made the point that young people now want to see a film, such as *Titanic* on first release. They are no longer willing to wait for it to come to their local picture house, but, with their ease of transport and better road communications, dash off to the first big city cinema showing the latest blockbuster.

Charles Scott, who ran a small cinema circuit for many years, following an earlier tradition set up by the Ellis family etc.

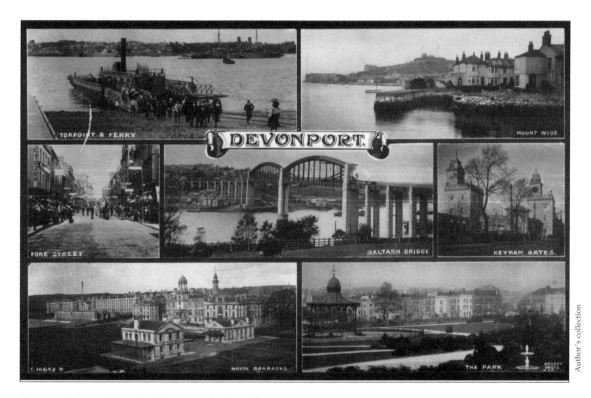

Devonport from an old postcard: it appears almost rural.

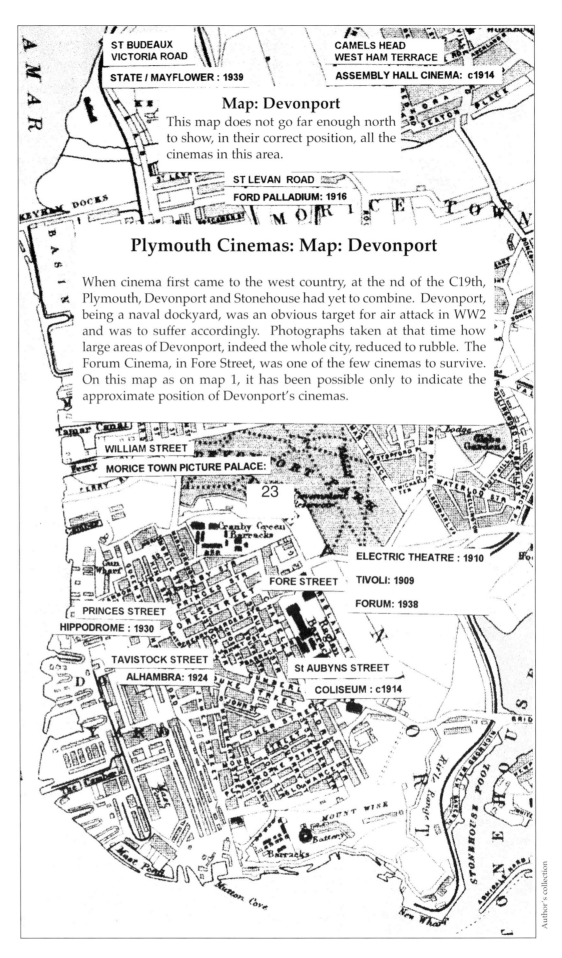

ST BUDEAUX
VICTORIA ROAD

STATE / MAYFLOWER : 1939

CAMELS HEAD
WEST HAM TERRACE

ASSEMBLY HALL CINEMA: c1914

Map: Devonport

This map does not go far enough north to show, in their correct position, all the cinemas in this area.

ST LEVAN ROAD

FORD PALLADIUM: 1916

Plymouth Cinemas: Map: Devonport

When cinema first came to the west country, at the nd of the C19th, Plymouth, Devonport and Stonehouse had yet to combine. Devonport, being a naval dockyard, was an obvious target for air attack in WW2 and was to suffer accordingly. Photographs taken at that time how large areas of Devonport, indeed the whole city, reduced to rubble. The Forum Cinema, in Fore Street, was one of the few cinemas to survive. On this map as on map 1, it has been possible only to indicate the approximate position of Devonport's cinemas.

WILLIAM STREET

MORICE TOWN PICTURE PALACE:

23

ELECTRIC THEATRE : 1910

FORE STREET

TIVOLI: 1909

FORUM: 1938

PRINCES STREET

HIPPODROME : 1930

TAVISTOCK STREET

ALHAMBRA: 1924

St AUBYNS STREET

COLISEUM : c1914

Assembly Hall Cinematograph Theatre   West Ham Terrace,
Combe Head   c1913-c1920s   [?]

This early cinema, of which a Mr Henry Slater is given as the owner (KD 1914 & 1919), opened just prior to the Great War (1914 - 1918) and ran through into the 1920s. Little seems to be known of this cinema. It was built at a time when cinema was becoming very popular, and many small and medium-sized cinemas came into being at this time. For various reasons, to be outlined in the next section, many did not survive the war years. To make the point, the KYB for 1914 lists ten cinemas in Devonport but the 1917 edition lists only five. There is no mention of this cinema in either edition.

Gaiety Appledore, showing the exterior of the projection box, with escape ladder.

Carlton, Okehampton, showing the projection box.

Coliseum Cinematograph Theatre   50, St Aubyn Street
c1912 - 1914   F

This is another cinema that appears in the 1914 KD. According to Mr Pat Ghillyer (CVA), who is now in his mid eighties and an authority on Plymouth's cinemas, this early cinema had a very short life, being burnt down about 1914. It then became the St Aubyn Garage. However the 1914 & 1917 editions of the KYB show a Theatre Coliseum in Devonport, seating 400 and run by M. Stein. KD give the proprietor as Mrs Annie Stein. I am tempted to suggest that these are one and the same, but I have no concrete evidence to back this suggestion. This area is now within the dockyard. Fire in a cinema was always a constant threat. The nitrate film stock in use at this time was highly flammable and was the cause of many cinema fires. The 1909 Cinematograph Act, which came into force on 1st January 1910, was aimed solely at protecting audiences from such fires. All projection booths had to be fire proof, with an external exit. Buckets of sand had to be placed in the auditorium. One council took this rather too far and insisted that a member of the local fire brigade, in full uniform, had to be in attendance at all performances. Though certainly not intended by the act itself, many local councils took this opportunity to look not just to the physical welfare of cinema patrons but also to their moral welfare. They used the act, in fact, to set up local censorship panels. It was this 'misuse' of the act that, as late as the 1930s, prevented the showing of *Frankenstein* in Exeter, though it was shown in Topsham. I am told that bus-loads of eager horror fans made the pilgrimage from Exeter to Topsham to see this classic of the horror genre.

Electric Theatre   Fore Street 1910 - 1941   Bz

This cinema, owned by the Electric Theatre Co, opened in 1910, and was therefore one of the earliest cinemas in the county. Having a captive audience

Electric, Devonport: an excellent interior.

Courtesy Tony Moss

was a sure way of filling the house and the coffers. This popular cinema was to survive the challenge of the Great War, the coming of sound and the Depression. What it could not survive was the blitz of 1941 when, along with other cinemas in the area and much of Devonport itself, it was destroyed. No trace now remains of the cinema.

Tivoli Cinematograph Theatre   8, Fore Street 1909 - 1941   Bz

The Tivoli, which opened in 1909, at 8 Fore Street Devonport was another cinema which survived the Great War, the coming of sound and the Depression, but seems to have been a casualty of the super-cinema boom in the 1930s. When in operation, it had a seating capacity of around 400, making it a typical medium-sized cinema of the period. It closed its doors in 1939. Then, like so much of Fore Street, it was destroyed in the blitz of April 1941. Photographs of Fore Street taken after the blitz show a sea of rubble in what had been a busy and important area of Devonport. It was only the more modern buildings, of steel and concrete construction, that were able to withstand both blast and fire, as for example the Forum Cinema, opened in 1938, also in Fore Street, still standing today, though no longer a cinema.

**Morice Town Picture Palace   32 William Street, Morice Town
c1914 - 1931   F**

Morice Town Picture Palace at 32 William Street opened in 1914 or perhaps a little before, with Maurice Lacy as the manager. It was a purpose-built cinema about which I have been unable to find any real details. It remained in operation throughout the Great War and went on into the sound era. However it did not last long as purveyor of 'talkies', as it burnt down in 1931.

Exeter Cinemas 1895 - 1914

City Palace / Lounge   79 Fore Street 1912 - 1932/1932 - 1942   Bz

This cinema, formerly a grocer's shop, at the top of Fore Street was opened in 1912 by a group of local businessmen. This was the pattern for many of the small and medium-sized cinemas throughout the county. It was not until the 1930s with the coming of the super cinemas that the pattern changed. However, in a largely rural county such as Devon, the local entrepreneur

A view of Fore Street Exeter. The City Palace/Lounge was situated in this area prior to the blitz.

Courtesy Express & Echo

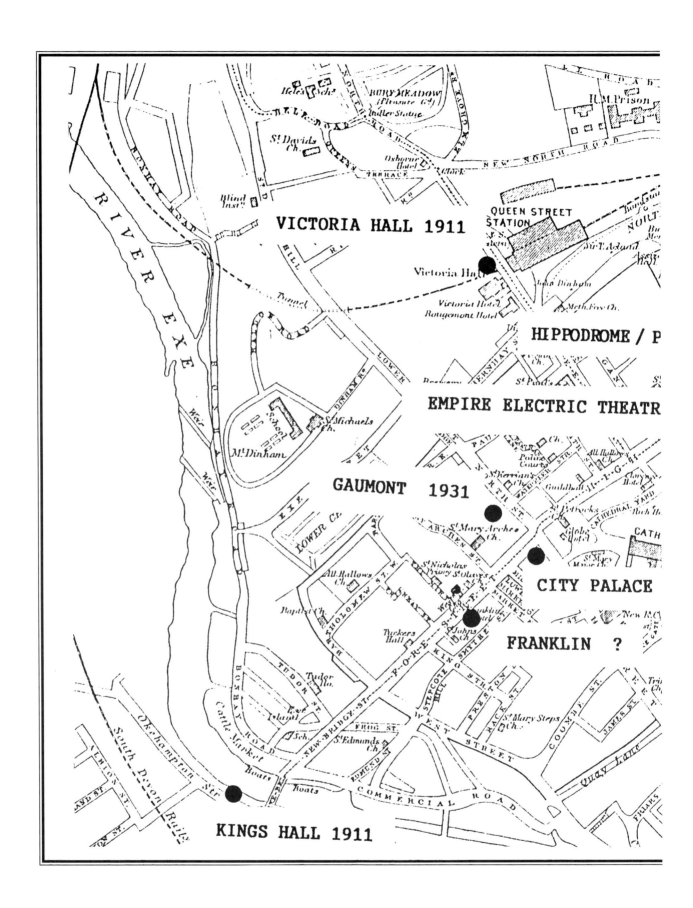

VICTORIA HALL 1911

QUEEN STREET
STATION

HIPPODROME / P

EMPIRE ELECTRIC THEATR

GAUMONT 1931

CITY PALACE

FRANKLIN ?

KINGS HALL 1911

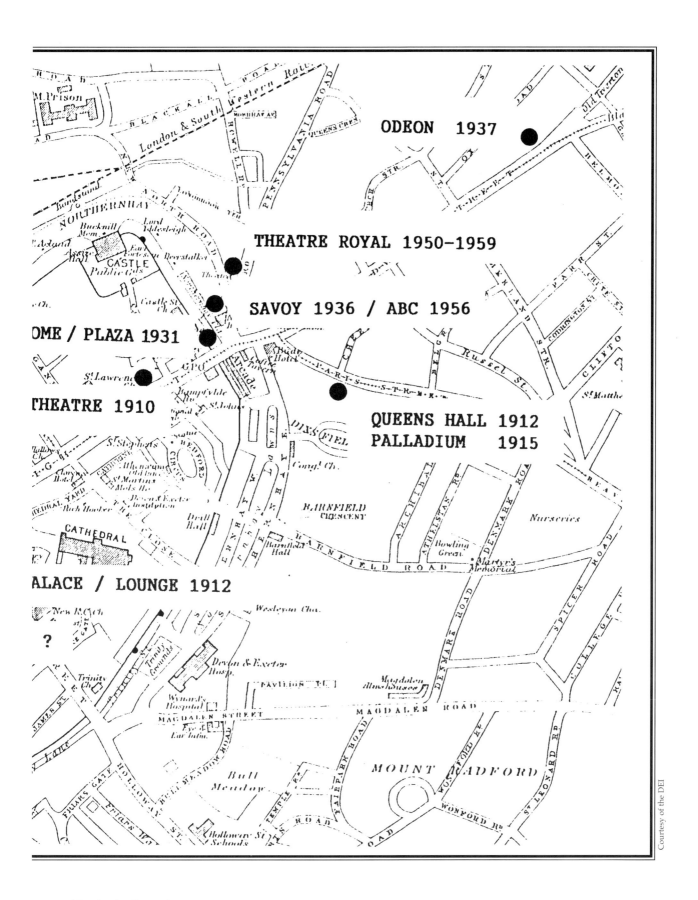

ODEON 1937

THEATRE ROYAL 1950–1959

SAVOY 1936 / ABC 1956

OME / PLAZA 1931

THEATRE 1910

QUEENS HALL 1912
PALLADIUM 1915

ALACE / LOUNGE 1912

?

Map showing Exeter cinemas.

remained an important figure in the provision of cinema entertainment. In fact, in one seaside town on the south Devon coast, the local owner enlarged his existing cinema in the hope of preventing a super-cinema being built in the town. Happily, the plan worked. The City Palace appears to have left little in the way of history and I have not even been able to find a photograph. In 1932 the name was changed to The Lounge. The *Express & Echo* (18.12.37) tells us that The Lounge ceased showing films in December 1937, almost certainly a casualty of the coming of the super-cinemas. It would appear the building was destroyed in the Blitz of 1942. No trace of the building can now be found. [1996]

Empire Electric Palace   248 High Street 1910 - 1937 cl   Bz 1942

The Empire Electric Palace, which was next to St. Lawrence's Church, was probably the first purpose-built cinema in Exeter. It was built on the site of what had been Wilson's restaurant. The cinema was owned by the Devon and Somerset Stores. It was opened in August 1910 when its prices were: adults: 3d, 6d and 1s., children: 2d and 3d. There were continuous performances from 2.30 pm to 10.30 pm. The entrance was at the screen end, not uncommon at that period. In its second week, it showed a sound version of the opera *Faust*. [Despite popular belief that sound was first introduced in 1927, when Jolson sang and spoke in *The Jazz Singer*, sound films were being made from the late 19th/early 20th century.]. Those Exonians who remember this cinema, speak of it as a 'flea-pit'. There seems to be some inverted snobbery here, as many cinemas gained this 'accolade', and there is pride in the voice of the ex-patron when telling of his or her visits to such a cinema. The Empire Electric Palace continued in operation throughout the Great War and survived the Depression, before it became a casualty of the super-cinema, only closing its doors in 1937. It would appear that the building was destroyed in the Blitz in 1942. A plaque marks the site of the former St. Lawrence's Church. [1996]

The Isca Collection, Exeter

Empire Electric Theatre, High Street, Exeter.
This very early cinema closed in 1937 and
the building was destroyed in the blitz.

Courtesy Tony Moss

The Interior of the Empire Electric.
Unfortunately I have no idea of
the actual date. Still, it is superb.

Courtesy Express & Echo

Palladium Outing, showing the lower façade of the Palladium Cinema.
This building was destroyed in 1941.

Queens Hall / Palladium
1912 - 1915 : 1915 - 1942

93-94 Paris Street
Bz

This was originally a dual-purpose building, serving both as a variety theatre and a cinema. The building was situated in Paris Street, approximately on the site of the Exeter Civic Centre building. It became the Palladium Cinema in 1915. As the Palladium it was an 800 seater cinema. Although destroyed in the Blitz of 1942 (a photograph of firemen fighting the fire at this building during the Blitz is included in Peter Thomas' book *Fire on the Wind* page 28), there is a suggestion that it was no longer being used as a cinema by this time, but as a food store. I have met two ex-fireman who were on duty in the city at the time of the blitz, and they both agree that this was, in fact, the case. A photograph of the first cinema works outing on 27 July 1930 appeared in the *Express & Echo* at that time. [1996]

Palladium, Programme for Way Down East 1920 : a typical piece of Griffith 'Victoriana' and very successful. Lillian Gish gave one of her most moving performances in this film, especially on the ice floe.

Franklin Picture Palace 101 Fore Street c1912 - 1923 BE

The Franklin remains something of a mystery. There was a Temperance Restaurant of that name at 101 Fore Street in the early years of the century. Hoskins tells us in *Two Thousand Years in Exeter,* that behind the restaurant was a hall of the same name showing films by 1912. This makes sense as at around this time the Temperance Movement supported cinema, the reason being that cinemas had no licence to sell alcohol and provided alternative entertainment to those establishments that were so licensed.

> *'The gradual decrease in drunkenness has been brought about by the open ing up of rational amusement such as the picture house.'*
> The Chief Constable of Edinburgh. 1917: Report to Commission -
> 'The Cinema: its Present Position and Future Possibilities.'

The Franklin Picture Palace appears both in KD and the KYB for 1914. But then, to add to the confusion, the KYB then lists the World Electric Picture Palace at the same address. Despite a diet of Charlie Chaplin films, then at their height of popularity, the cinema closed in 1923. When I visited the building in 1995, it was then The Remnant Shop, where an assistant remembered it in its days as a cinema. Since then The Remnant Shop has closed and the building has been remodelled and opened as a Australian pub called Walkabout. [1996 - 1998]

The site of the Franklin Cinema, Fore Street which has changed again since this photograph was taken [1997] and is now a public house.

Victoria Hall, 1910, a typical 'multi-use' building that was destroyed by fire [nothing to do with its role as a part-time cinema] in 1919. Never rebuilt.

Victoria Hall   32 Queen Street 1910 - 1919   F:D

Victoria Hall was situated at 32, Queen Street and was a popular venue for many and varied events, films included. I have copies of programmes for performances of the *'Messiah'* by the Exeter Choral Society here on Wednesday 13th December 1911, and the *'Grand Orchestral and Vocal Concerts'* (Conductor - Mr A Norman Kendall) on Friday 6th October 1916. From the same source, Mr Dick Passmore, I have a photograph taken in 1910 showing a fire behind the Victoria Hall at a local timber yard. Films seem to have been shown here, as part of its varied programme, from sometime prior to 1911. Hoskins, in his *Two Thousand Years In Exeter,* mentions seasonal visits to Victoria Hall by West's Animated Pictures . Tragically the building was burnt down in 1919. A drawing of the building appears in Peter Thomas' book *The Changing Face of Exeter* page 109. [1996]

Kings Hall, a multi-use building that became a full time cinema, was then used for war work during WW2, and is now the Riverside Christian Centre.

Kings Hall   13 -14 Okehampton Street 1912 - 1936   BE

This building on Okehampton Street remains but is much altered.. It was opened by the mayor in 1912 as a multi-purpose building, in which the showing of films was only a part of its function. It was converted to a cinema in 1921. Stuart Smith in his book *The Theatres and Cinemas of Exeter* tells us that the Kings Hall was the first cinema in Exeter to show talking films, in this case *The Donnovan Affair* in 1929. This cinema was yet another hall to fall to the advent of the city's super-cinemas, closing in 1937. During the war years it was used by J. Wippell and Co. Later it became a store for Ferodo and at present it is run as a night club. (Since the above was written, the building has changed use yet again to become the 'Riverside Christian Centre' - August 1998). A view of the Kings Hall, showing surrounding blitz damage, appears in the Peter Thomas book *Fire in the Wind* page 37. [17.11.96]

Other Venues in use for showing Films in Exeter at this Period:

As has already been mentioned in the introduction, the showing of films was not confined to purpose-built cinemas at this period. Almost all music halls and even some theatres were including the showing of films as part of the entretainment on offer. The same is true of shows on the pier. A well-known postcard shows advertisements for film shows on the pier at Weston-super-Mare at this time. The 1917 edition of KYB notes 'seaside cinema' at the Pier Pavilions in Exmouth, Plymouth, Torquay and Paignton.

In Exeter, the Theatre Royal, the Hippodrome (later converted to the Plaza Cinema) and the Barnfield Hall are all listed in the KYB 1914. Another mystery is the listing of a Royal in Longbrook Street. This is given as a 1300 seater belonging to 'Exeter Theatre Ltd'. Surely this must be the Theatre Royal under another name?

The Pier at Torquay. Such seaside venues brought early cinema to the holiday crowds, along with the fair ground examples already shown.

Exmouth Cinemas 1895 - 1914

Savoy / Picture Palace   Rolle Street   c1914 -   CWC

The Exmouth Picture Palace opened in Rolle Street circa 1914 and appears to have been the first permanent home for cinema in the town. It seems that there have only ever been four cinemas in Exmouth. This being so, it is obvious that these cinemas have, as is not uncommon, changed their names at least once over the years. One source states that this cinema was originally the Town Hall Cinema, which then became the Capitol and only much later became the Savoy. The Picture Palace appears in KD in 1914 and again in 1919 and 1923 but is not found in the 1935 edition, when the Savoy Cinema is given at that address, and the Savoy also appears in the 1939 edition of that work. The KYB for 1914 gives an Electric Palace, no address, owned by Mr Leon Vint: I assume this to be the same cinema. The cinema has had many owners over the years. In 1914 the owners were, according to KD, F.W. & E.A. Headington, but by 1919, E.A. Headington is no longer mentioned. In 1923 W.J.A. Bayley was the owner, with John E. Crews and John Brooks being the owners in 1935 and 1939 respectively. During those years, 1935 to 1939, Frederick B. Hall was the manager. In the 1960s and 1970s the Savoy formed part of Charles Scott's circuit and, at the time of writing (1998), was one of four cinemas in Devon run by Mr Peter Hoare. The cinema entrance and foyer form part of a block of buildings, which have an Edwardian look to them. It is only when looking at the rear of the building that one gets any clue to its real function. I understand from Mr Hoare that a bomb fell on the cinema during the war but, fortunately, it did not explode. The Savoy is now the only cinema in Exmouth, all its competitors having closed, though two of the three buildings still survive; the fourth was demolished in the latter half of the 1990s. [9.10.96]

Savoy, Exmouth. Very much part of this Edwardian block, and not so out of place as cinemas often were.

Savoy, Exmouth. Interior, when the cinema had only the traditional one screen.

The Cinema, High Street, Honiton. A typical 'hidden cinema' which makes life difficult for the cinema researcher.

Honiton Cinemas 1895 - 1914

Honiton Cinema   High Street   c1914 - c1930   BE

Here we have a classic example of the 'hidden' cinema. Walking past the present shop at 62, High Street there is nothing to suggest that this was once Honiton's picture house. However a postcard of Honiton High Street c1920, which Mr Gerald Gosling has kindly allowed me to copy, clearly shows the building in its cinematic role. The KYB for 1917 gives the seating as 250. The Cinema, which was its name as well as its function, was operational by 1914 and continued through to the 1930s. Upstairs in the modern shop, 'Rebecca & Ryans', are traces of ornamental plaster work which would seem to have been part of the décor of the cinema auditorium ceiling. Similar plaster work can be seen in many early cinemas, a legacy from the music hall / theatre architecture

The same scene but with the cinema:1920

of a previous generation. However, it could well be the remains of an even earlier ceiling harking back to its more domestic role. I understand that, after its days as a purveyor of Hollywood dreams, the building had a very varied career, at one time becoming the local ambulance station. The Devonia, which opened at the bottom of the town at 205, High Street, in the 1930s, was surely the cause of this closure. Photographs of both these cinemas appear in *Around Honiton* by Les Berry and Gerald Gosling, pages 21 and 30. [16.4.96]. There has now been another change of use, which I noted when visiting Honiton last year. [1999]

The Northfield /New/ etc, Ilfracombe. The façade of the Rechabite Hall is unchanged from the day in 1911 when the upper storey first became a cinema.

Ilfracombe Cinemas 1895 - 1914

Northfield Picture Palace   Northfield Road   1911 - 1951   BE

This was another building that gave no clue to its use as a cinema. Yet it had been in operation since 1911, opening its doors for the first time on Saturday April 11th of that year. In fact, it occupied the upper floor of the Rechabite Hall and the Rechabite temperance movement continued to use the lower floors after the upper floor was converted to a cinema. This could be another example of the link between temperance and the cinema. The cinema remained in constant use from 1911 until it closed on October 1st 1951. Though constant in its use, it was not constant in name. In 1915 the Cinema was renamed the Electric Theatre, changing in 1916 to the Empire Cinema. It remained such until 1932 when it became The Plaza. After only a year it changed again in 1933 to become The New Cinema and thus it remained until it closed in 1951. The building still stands in Northfield Road, looking totally unchanged, externally, from that day in 1911 when the movies first found a permanent home in Ilfracombe. The KYB of 1914 gives the seating capacity as 375. In 1917 the owner is given as A.O. Ellis. [17.7.97] I heard this year [2000] that the building has been up for sale, but I have no confirmation of this at present.

The Palace   25 High Street 1913 - 1926

This early cinema opened on Thursday 10th July 1913, only two years after the Picture Palace. Prior to its use as a cinema, this building had been a public house and snooker hall. On Friday May 2nd 1913, the *Ilfracombe Gazette &*

Observer carried both a drawing of the proposed new cinema and café and an article outlining both the exterior and interior of the building.

'*Bath stone facings will be used in alterations to the façade and the exposed woodwork will be in mahogany, thus ensuring a very handsome appearance. The paving of the entrance lobby will be black and white marble. The interior of the building will be decorated in fibrous plaster and we are given to understand that the furnishing and the general decoration scheme is of a character that will fully justify the title given to the building.*

The auditorium is very lofty and particular attention has been paid to the ventilation, which is designed to give a cool and comfortable hall under all conditions. [See Torbay Cinema entry for more information on this aspect of cinema architecture.] The ground floor and balcony will be raked and, as there are no pillars, everyone will have an uninterrupted view of the stage. The safety and comfort of patrons has received first consideration in arranging the ground plan. The main entrance is by double doors leading almost directly off the street, thus avoiding long corridors and stairs with their attendant dangers. In all, four exits are provided to High Street and Avenue Road and in these all steps have been avoided, a most important feature. Above the entrance, reached by a fireproof stair, is situated the café and tea room which will be open to both the patrons of the theatre and the public. Immediately behind this and leading from it is the balcony. As will be seen from the brief preliminary description we are able to give, the theatre will prove a great addition to the attractions of the town and will be of a class seldom met with in a town of this size. Arrangements have been made to open the premises in early July'.

The cinema was opened on Thursday 10th July 1913.

I have quoted from this article at length for several reasons. Firstly, because it is typical of many articles, describing the building or opening of new cinemas, written during the first four decades of the twentieth century. Secondly, because it gives a clear picture of what cinema owners saw as important when setting out to provide a town with a new venue for movie entertainment. Also it is interesting to note that the word cinema does not appear: everywhere the building is described as a theatre and the screen area is referred to as the stage, but perhaps the most interesting point to note is the importance given to safety. In the 19th century, theatre fires had been only too common and, in Devon, memories of the tragic fire at the Exeter Theatre Royal in September 1887 must

Advert from local paper showing the cinema as part of the Albany Ward circuit.

Memorial in Higher Cemetery, Exeter, to the dead of the Exeter Theatre fire in1887, which was to result in a far greater safety factor in places of public entertainment.

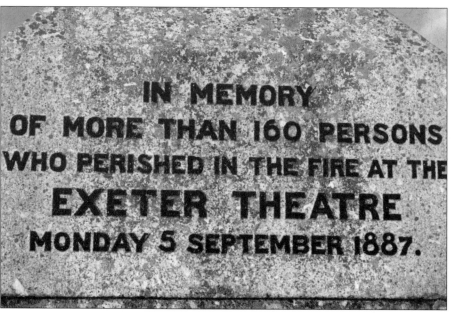

IN MEMORY
OF MORE THAN 160 PERSONS
WHO PERISHED IN THE FIRE AT THE
EXETER THEATRE
MONDAY 5 SEPTEMBER 1887.

still have been very much in people's minds. Early cinemas were, from the very beginning, even more prone to such disasters and this led in 1909 to the Cinematograph Act already mentioned. In an article in the same newspaper, devoted to the opening of the Palace Cinema in July 1913, the safety angle is again to the fore: *'The premises have been entirely constructed on the latest principles to form a comfortable, roomy and <u>safe hall</u>. Attention having been given to every point that can ensure the <u>welfare of the patrons</u> . Seating accommodation has been provided for 400 in the area and 100 in the balcony and there is ample standing room beside.'* [my underlining]

This cinema was short-lived, closing its doors for the last time on Saturday 13th March 1926. The site was taken over by Woolworth's Ltd. who opened a store there in 1927. This in turn closed in 1988 and was re-opened as a Superdrug store. [1997]

This stone was re-dedicated in 1987 by the Regiment, and a radio play by a local playwright re-told this harrowing story.

Newton Abbot Cinemas 1895 - 1914

Imperial Electric Theatre   **Queen Street Pre 1914 - ??**   **FE**

This is one of at least four cinemas to have operated in the town over the years. This *appears* to have been the first, though it is possible that the Alexandra may have some claim to that honour. It is often difficult, if not impossible, to find evidence from the earliest days of moving pictures to prove just who *did* show the very first 'flickers' in town.

The Imperial was certainly a going concern by 1914 when it appears in KD and the KYB. The imposing façade of the building still stands in Queen Street, though the interior of what was the cinema has been totally changed. An early photograph of Queen Street showing the Imperial Cinema, when compared

The Imperial Cinema, Newton Abbot. Sadly, only the façade of this building now remains, but the remains are very impressive.

with a 1996 photograph of the same street, demonstrates how little the street has altered over the years. (The first-mentioned photograph will be found in Roger Jones' 1979 publication *A Book of Newton Abbot*. There is also an early photograph showing the present Alexandra cinema prior to its film-showing days.) [2.10.96]

An early photograph, taken when the cinema was newly opened, shows the building and street little different from that taken in 1997.

Courtesy Roger Jones

Picture Palace:	Newton Abbot	[?]

There is no address or information, other than the name, given in the KYB for 1914. This could be the name in use at that time, when showing films, for what is now the Alexandra. We know from Mr Peter Hoare that the Alexandra was showing films in the silent period.

Paignton Cinemas: 1895 - 1914

Early advertisement c1914

Courtesy J. J. Mann

Paignton (Torbay) Picture House   Torbay Road   c1909 - 1999

There were originally some serious doubts as to when, exactly, this cinema first opened to the public. I have copies of plans that are dated 1913, but this was thought possibly to represent an enlargement or a re-building. Since I began this account, further plans have come to light dated 1909. This beautiful little cinema was under threat of closure for the whole period of the research, finally closing on the 25th September 1999. On that day a Radio 4 programme, telling the history of the cinema, was recorded on site and broadcast in the series *"Flicks in the Sticks"* early in 2000. The building is brick throughout, unlike many other cinemas with their imposing façades fronting a far less imposing auditorium of concrete block and asbestos roof. The interior, basically unchanged since it opened, is a delight to the eye. The architecture of the interior is remarkably similar to that of the Electric Portobello Road [1905] and the former Andrews New Picture Palace [1914] in Union Street, Plymouth. The latter was demolished to make way for the Gaumont Palace in 1931.

The following account of the early history of the Torbay Picture House was taped when the Exeter Branch of the Devonshire Association visited the cinema on 17th July 1998. The account gives not only facts on the structure but also

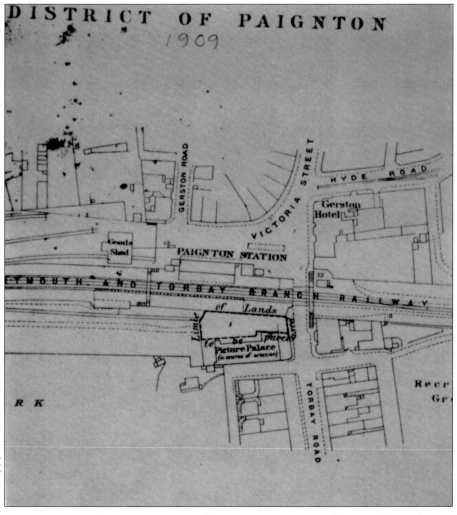

Courtesy J.J. Mann

Plan showing site for the cinema dated 1909

Courtesy J.J. Mann

a vivid picture of cinema-going in the very early days of this new form of mass entertainment. The speaker was Mr J.J.Mann, who was then the manager of the cinema. The session was held on the balcony of the cinema.

Early seating plan, showing three, not two, private boxes.

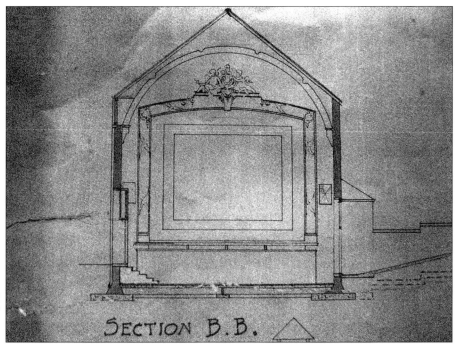

Courtesy J.J. Mann

SECTION B.B.

Paignton Picture House, Paignton. Elevation of the proscenium arch. Plans dated 1913.

Paignton Picture House. The proscenium arch and screen, 1912/13, from a glass slide found during renovation work at the cinema in recent years.

'Any Agatha Christie book where the Palace Cinema turns up in the story, this is the place it was based on. The hall [auditorium] was completed between 1907 and 1910, thereby it's got the record of being the oldest cinema in Western Europe. The décor is exactly the same as it always was, the colour scheme is the same. You're all too young to remember a lot of the silent films, obviously, but the mask you see there is Douglas Fairbanks as Moses, and the crests are the old film company crests. The circle itself, this part, has got an interesting history. When this place was built it was called the 'Electric Bioscopic Exhibition Centre with Entertainment Suitable for Ladies'. When it opened, for the first five years it was gentlemen on that side [right facing screen] and ladies on this side. The word cinema didn't exist, and the people who came here first, if you can imagine their backgrounds, they would have been working for the local farmers, they may have been tradesmen. They were obviously totally amazed when they came into a place like this and saw a moving picture. It would have been a show with slides, interspersed with small films of about 20 minutes duration. The first films to be shown here were actually four minutes each, with slides in between them, beautiful Victorian slides, hand coloured. You would see about 6 or 7 slides, you'd have a programme, and the orchestra would play: a 21-piece orchestra which opened here. Later you will see the receipts for that - how much they got.

['Received of the Paignton Picture House Ltd: the sum of £5 : 5 : 0 for Orchestral performances for the week ending 3rd November 1917'. & 'Received of the Paignton Picture house Ltd: the sum of £13 : 0 : 0 being 1 week's salary of the Orchestra for the week ending 30th July 1921'.]

Receipt, dated July 1921: one of several such receipts, some dating from the early days of the cinema. Sound brought mass unemployment to cinema musicians throughout the world.

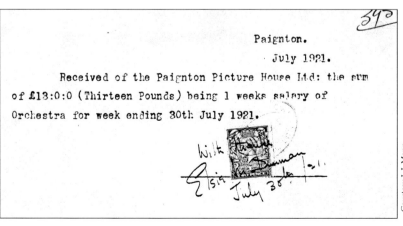

There would be slides, local views; then that would stop and they would actually show a moving picture. The first moving picture ever shown here was A Rough Sea at Brighton *- four minutes - and then the next was* A Train Going Into Waterloo. *When they actually put the train on, going into the station - so our records tell us - about six women fainted. Of course, they'd seen nothing like it before. They had no home entertainment, no radio, no television. The gramophone was really just catching on in the 1900s.*

What we are going to attempt to do now is to recreate on the screen the original picture size, the original picture colour which was sepia colour. And we have Pam at the piano, the only theatre pianist, maybe, in the world. So bear with us for five minutes and we will take you on a journey right back to the 1900s.

The cinema pianist struck up with *If I had a Talking Picture of You*, house lights dimmed, the curtains parted and we were treated to a Snub Pollard silent film with full musical accompaniment: for a time we all were back in the golden days at the birth of cinema. [Snub Pollard was an Australian comedian who worked in early slap-stick silents in America. Later he did bit-parts in many films, his last appearance was in *A Pocketful of Miracles* in 1961].

Following this film, Mr Mann was asked how he became involved with the cinema and the film trade:

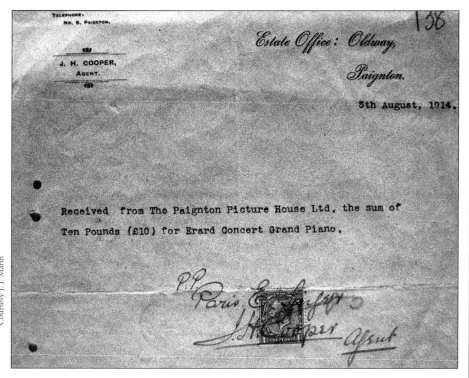

Courtesy J. J. Mann

Receipt for grand piano, a gift from Paris Singer to the cinema. The Singer family settled in Paignton and did a great deal for the town over the years.

Author's collection

JJ Mann in the cinema office, looking at the 1915 cinema diary which, on this page, shows the Chaplin film Tillie's Punctured Romance. *Looking down on the scene is Mr Drew, builder of the cinema.*

'*I started as a clapper boy at 14/- a week. We had local film studios in Paignton then. Archway Films, a very famous company in its day, and British Lion were based here. I knew this place then because we used to bring films here to see the rushes, to see what it would be like on the big screen, and I never forgot the place. It's come in and out of my life at regular periods of time. It has an enormously colourful history.*

The gentleman who built it was a local builder called Drew; Mr Drew and they [his company] only finished operating in 1975. They maintained the building right up to 1975. The late Mr Drew, Great Grandad Drew as he was known in the town... Our local business men, one of whom was Mr Lambshead, said, 'Let's build a

Author's collection

The former 'Archway Studios' at the Oldway Mansion.The Rotunda became Studio 1 which retains,to this day, the sound-proofing on the walls.

Author's collection

The Archway Studios restaurant, now past its sell-by date. Early photographs of Oldway show the 'greenhouses' in all their glory. This section had been used by Isadora Duncan as part of the swimming suite.

Picture Palace, whatever it is'. They hadn't got a clue what they were going to do - they didn't know anything about it. But they all trooped off to the Gaumont in Paris and had a look at that, and when they came back Mr Drew started to build the place. And obviously he thought it must be something like a Music-Hall, hence the baroque look to the design. Then he came to build the circle, and the owners, [who] had been travelling around looking at other elegant buildings, wanted this curved sweep. Our local builders had never built anything like that before because they had just built straight balconies in Wesleyan chapels and churches. He thought, how do we do this? ... he constructed a massive iron framework and built the deck of this beautiful balcony. And he - this is absolutely authentic, a great grand-daughter told me this - he worried and worried and worried and thought, I must get this right and make sure it's safe. So he paid 500 workmen a penny each to come in the morning, each carrying a one hundredweight sack of lime, and stand shoulder to shoulder. He tied a fishing line from the bottom of the beam to the floor to see if there was any deflection. There was. So he dou-

bled everything in the building specs. (sic). He reinforced the walls with iron bars every 5 inches through the brick and doubled this up to make sure. Now when we have our survey with the modern seismograph equipment and every thing else you have got today, our local borough engineer has calculated that you could put two railway engines in this circle. [The Cinema] was built on a salt marsh and it's got no foundations in the true sense of the word. How Mr Drew achieved this - he was building in Paignton, and Paignton is all reclaimed land, it was just swamp land. The

Balcony end of the auditorium, showing the projection ports and the two private boxes.

Showing Station Road and the Broadmead Hotel, which was demolished to make way for the cinema.

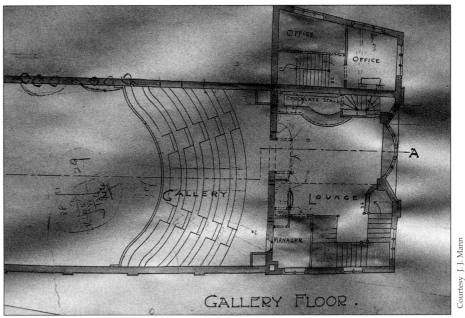

Plan of the gallery floor from the 1913 plans.

traditional method of doing it [was that] *they used to grow vast areas of things called withies and apparently they used to cut the stuff, weave huge mats of it, put it with the local clay from Newton Abbot and let it dry in huge slabs, and place these on top of the salt beds, layer after layer after layer. Then they would use about ten layers of railway sleepers that they bought from the Great Western Railway, which of course were pickled in creosote and on top of that he put 5 feet of reinforced concrete bed with iron bars. Now that's being very safe. The building has moved one eleventh of an inch that side since it was built and it's been through the blitz, the bombing, the war, traffic and the modern age.*

These arches [pointing to the ornate ceiling] ...are actually made of oak. There are iron A- frames behind those. The roof is Welsh slate and there's never been anything changed. The fancy work is what they call 'Stick & Rag'; and once again they used withies, pounded up to almost a powdered state and with... butter muslin they mixed it with Plaster of Paris and they would make all this beautiful décor in that. Many years ago, in West Country Television days, we were making a documentary about Devon crafts and I had the privilege of meeting a plasterer, he was 87, who [as

Screen end. The lights were added in 1921.

Private box (a five seater) used by the Edgar Wallace family. The two seater was used by Paris Singer and Isadora Duncan.

an apprentice]*worked on this* [building]. *He said that they could only work for 2 days on this fancy work because it was so repetitive and then they would have to do something else, leave it for 2 days then come back to it; because they would just slow up and get slap happy and Mr Drew wouldn't have any bad workmanship. He would put them on something else and then bring them back again. The whole building was built in 12 months.*

[Question: ' What is the actual date of opening? The plans that I borrowed and copied are dated 1913.']

I should explain this. In 1913 the final front of the building was completed and this was the office block on the side. So that was the building in its complete form. Before that, the hall [auditorium] was built first and the Broadmead Hotel -where my colleague is standing [points to the rear wall of the balcony] *would be the back wall of the Broadmead Hotel, which went forward* [from there]. *They kept the Broadmead and people would come through the front door of the Broadmead and into the hall. They obviously had to make money* [from the hotel] *because they had mortgaged themselves ... to pay for this. They were relatively young men taking a chance. So they*

Close-up of the balcony, showing some of the "Rag & Stick work" decoration, see text for details.

Receipt for film of the 'East Coast Bombardment' dated 19th December 1914.

Picture of the ceiling, showing the ceiling grills for the air conditioning, as described by J J Mann in his history of the cinema given to the D. A.

ran the hotel till the last minute, built the hall and the private boxes and then they took the hotel down in half and then the other half. The final completion date, when the Paignton Picture House was formed, was 1913. [I have seen the minutes of the meeting (1913) when the cinema was officially formed; these are now held by Mr Robert Letcher of Paignton - author's note.] *But it was operating before then as the Paignton Bioscopic Exhibition Centre with Entertainment Suitable for Ladies. We think that that was probably 1909, because a lot of the plans are dated 1909, which we have found since you saw the other plans......They didn't really pay for this place till about 1929 when the last debts were paid. They took a chance. It must have been a nice day and age, if you had the get up and go to take chances because you weren't quite as restricted then. The other thing is they had terrific licensing problems. There were objections to this place being built by certain elements, the clergy etc. The Wesleyans didn't like it much in those days, why I don't know. So what did they* [The Paignton Picture House] *do ? They said, 'Look your place isn't very big or very palatial, you can have this place on Sundays'. So when this place was closed on Sundays, it was the Wesleyan Chapel for quite some time. Then all of a sudden they changed their views. The first manager was called Mr Fred Bunting, now there's a name for you. The orchestra was quite good and we have a memo from the Leader of the orchestra to Mr Fred Bunting complaining that the operator* [projectionist]*was running the Tom Mix films too fast and if he doesn't stop, the Leader of the orchestra is going to walk out, as he can't keep up with it. It was a hand turned machine and he got excited and cranked too fast and the orchestra couldn't keep up.*

[These grills up here (in the ceiling]) are presumably for ventilation?]
Yes, it was one of the first buildings, I would think, in the country, to have true air conditioning. The air was pumped in, filtered and then taken out through the top. Originally we know there were chandeliers hung, but we have no idea of the design yet. The house lights [down in the auditorium] *are a bit later, 1921, very much art-deco. They were made by the local blacksmith, as opposed to farrier, and made in tin. When they were put up, everybody complained and said 'Oh ***, the modern generation, what are they doing?' Now they are collectors' items in their own right.*

[Have you any idea how much it cost to build ?]
£4,000. In fact I will now show you some of the bills. This will amaze you.
Various documents were shown to the group relating to the building and running of the cinema. [T: 17.7.98]

Close up of the ceiling grills, Paignton Picture House.

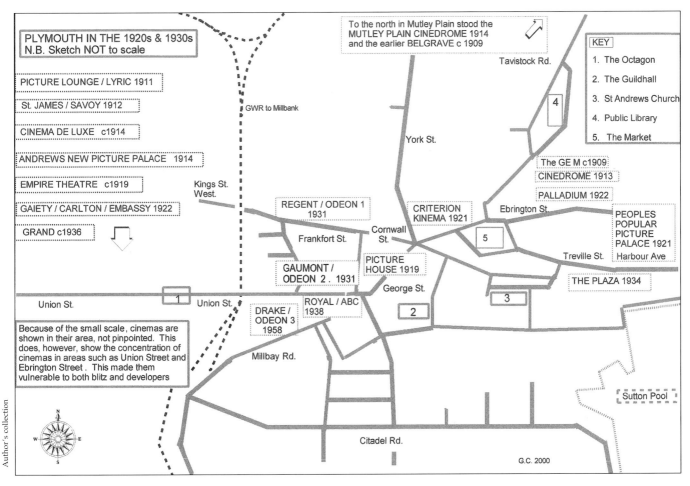

PLYMOUTH IN THE 1920s & 1930s
N.B. Sketch NOT to scale

PICTURE LOUNGE / LYRIC 1911

St. JAMES / SAVOY 1912

CINEMA DE LUXE c1914

ANDREWS NEW PICTURE PALACE 1914

EMPIRE THEATRE c1919

GAIETY / CARLTON / EMBASSY 1922

GRAND c1936

Because of the small scale, cinemas are shown in their area, not pinpointed. This does, however, show the concentration of cinemas in areas such as Union Street and Ebrington Street. This made them vulnerable to both blitz and developers

To the north in Mutley Plain stood the MUTLEY PLAIN CINEDROME 1914 and the earlier BELGRAVE c 1909

KEY
1. The Octagon
2. The Guildhall
3. St Andrews Church
4. Public Library
5. The Market

Tavistock Rd.

GWR to Millbank

York St.

Kings St. West.

REGENT / ODEON 1 1931

Frankfort St.

GAUMONT / ODEON 2. 1931

Cornwall St.

PICTURE HOUSE 1919

George St.

CRITERION KINEMA 1921

Ebrington St.

The GE M c1909
CINEDROME 1913
PALLADIUM 1922

PEOPLES POPULAR PICTURE PALACE 1921 Harbour Ave

Treville St.

THE PLAZA 1934

Union St.

Union St.

DRAKE / ODEON 3 1958

ROYAL / ABC 1938

Millbay Rd.

Citadel Rd.

Sutton Pool

G.C. 2000

Author's collection

C19th Map of Plymouth showing the centre of the city which contained the majority of cinemas and which suffered most in the blitz.

Plymouth Cinemas 1895 - 1914

It is difficult to find conclusive evidence for the earliest cinema in Plymouth, as it is for any town. Many early venues were in the nature of 'one night stands' which have left no trace. The KYB for 1914 gives 6 cinemas operating in Plymouth at that date as does KD ; unfortunately they are not the same six. The Theatre Elite, (11, Ebrington Street) and the St. James Picture Hall (108 Union Street) are the only ones the two lists have in common. The KYB also lists : Electric Theatre (St. John's), Empire Electric Theatre, Hippodrome, and the Theatre De Luxe; while KD lists: Andrews New Picture Palace (151 Union Street - later the Gaumont), Belgrave Electric Theatre, Cinedrome (57, Ebrington Street) and Mutley Cinedrome (56, Mutley Plain). At this early date I have found KD to be the more useful as it gives fuller information for each venue. In later years the KYB proves the more helpful when it began to include such information as addresses, seating, prices, opening patterns, owners and even the equipment used in projection and sound.

The Gem   Ebrington Street c1905 - ?   [?]

One of the earliest cinemas, of which there are no more than hints, was the Gem in Ebrington Street which seems to have been in operation about 1905. No more information appears to be available. It has been suggested, though I have found no evidence to support the theory, that a later cinema was to be found on the same site, possibly the Elite.

St. James Hall, which was later demolished to make way for the Savoy cinema. Note the performances on Xmas Day with Andrews Pictures.

Picture Lounge / Lyric　　　34 Union Street 1911 - 1916　　　[?]

In 1911 the Picture Lounge, later re-named the Lyric, opened at 34 Union Street, Stonehouse. This short- lived cinema then became the Lyric Dance Hall.

Belgrave Electric Theatre　　2 Belgrave Road 1912 - 1983　　BE

Another very early purpose-built cinema was the Belgrave Electric Theatre at 2 Belgrave Road, Mutley Plain, which opened in 1912. In 1914 the lessees were Montague Gilpin & Alfred Williams. Previously the site had been connected with horses, being at one stage the tramway stables. It is an imposing building even now, which gives some clue to the importance that cinema had attained even at this early date, and the exterior looks much as it must have done in its heyday. I understand that the interior has been much changed, and is now a snooker hall. When I visited the Belgrave in 1997 there was some doubt as to its future when the present lease runs out. There was talk of the site being used as a car park ! [25.6.97]

The Belgrave Cinema, Mutley Plain. An early, much loved cinema, still remembered with affection, as is Walter, who seemed to do everything at the cinema.

Cinedrome, Ebrington Street. This façade is all that is left of this cinema following the blitz. It could also be the site of The Gem, another early cinema in this street.

The Cinedrome   57 Ebrington Street   1913 - 1941.   FE

The Cinedrome was opened at 57 Ebrington Street by the proprietor William Linsdell, who also owned the Mutley Plain Cinedrome in Mutley Plain. Badly damaged in the blitz of 1941, only the façade now remains. It is an interesting, though not a particularly imposing façade, being only a single storey. It is no longer possible to gain any impression of the rest of the building. The current owner, Mr John Milton, was unable to give me any further information on this early cinema, but kindly provided photographs of the façade when it was last stripped for re-painting. [16.1.97]

Empire   40 Union Street   1910 -   1941   Bz

This very early cinema, which opened in August 1910, was to survive the Great War, the Depression and the coming of sound in the late 1920s. Sadly it was one of many cinemas in both Plymouth and Devonport to succumb to the blitz in the

Second World War. Union Street was a favourite location for cinemas over the years and in consequence the heavy bombing of the area saw the demise of several 'picture palaces' besides the Empire. I am indebted to Pat Ghillyer for bringing this cinema to my attention. So far no picture has come to light.

Cinema de Luxe   10 Union Street   c1914 - c1927   Bz?

In 1914 the Cinema de Luxe opened in Union Street but I have been unable to find out any further information on this building. The approximate date of closing suggests that it may have been one of the many casualties of the sound revolution: the Warner Brothers' part-talkie *The Jazz Singer* opened in New York on 6th October 1927.

The coming of sound, with the expense of wiring the cinema and other extra costs, was to cause the closure of many of the smaller cinemas where profits were too small to cover the cost of conversion. It has been estimated that 'talkies' cost up to a £100 per week more to show than silents, and the cost of film hire had risen steeply. These are the figures given for the Granada cinema chain and although they would have been less for smaller halls, so also would the profit margin involved.

Mutley Plain Cinedrome   56 Mutley Plain 1914 - c1927   [?]

The Mutley Plain Cinedrome had a chequered career. Opened in 1914 as the Mutley Plain Cinedrome, it changed its name in 1925 to the Roseville. This was but a short interlude, as in 1926 the name changed again to the Argyll. As the Argyll, this cinema lasted for only about a year, closing circa 1927, probably another casualty of the coming of sound.

Andrews New Picture Palace   151 Union Street   1910 / 14 - 1931   D

This cinema was a 1500 seater with a barrel-roofed interior typical of the period. Similar interiors can be seen in the Torbay Cinema, Paignton and the Electric Cinema, Portobello Road, London. The building lasted until 1931 when it was demolished to make way for the new Gaumont Palace. This later building still stands though it is now a night club. The rest of the history of this site will be included at the appropriate stage.

Richard Barthelmess & Mary Pickford, two very early stars of the silver screen. Both worked for D.W. Griffith.

On the wall of this later building is a memorial plaque to the great British cinematograph pioneer, William Friese-Greene, who had a shop on the site in the late nineteenth century. Friese-Greene was born in Bristol in 1855 and educated at the Blue Coat School in Clifton. A very successful still photographer, he spent some £10,000 of his own money in developing 'moving' pictures. The cost of his pioneer research was more than he could afford. He spent time in prison for debt and when he died, on May 5th 1921, he was found to have 1/10d in his pocket, the cost of a cinema seat. This was all the money that he possessed. He died having just given a speech to the cinema trade at the Connaught in London. This information is taken from an article *How Films Began* by his son, Claude Friese-Greene, which appeared in *The World Film Encyclopaedia* published in 1933.

Sidmouth Cinemas 1895 - 1914

Cinema Picture Palace   Fore Street 1911 / 12 - 1929   BE

The Cinema Picture Palace opened in circa 1911-12 and it appears in KD in 1914. However, this was not the first home of the 'flickers' in Sidmouth. Prior to the opening of the Cinema Picture Palace, films had been shown in both the

Andrews New Picture Palace. This early cinema was demolished to make way for the Gaumont Palace in Union Street. The Gaumont building is still there.

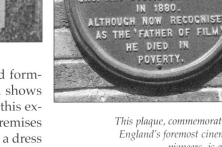

This plaque, commemorating one of England's foremost cinematograph pioneers, is adjacent to the ex-Gaumont.

Manor Hall and then in the Drill Hall. It appears that this cinema had formerly been the Belle Vue Restaurant. One photograph that I have seen shows the cinema surrounded by water in the floods of 1924. When I visited this ex-cinema [22.6.98] I was amazed at what remained of the interior. The premises is now, and has been since the Knight family opened their shop in 1938, a dress shop and drapers. The present Mr Knight gave me a guided tour of the shop and had this to say about the old cinema:

'It was opened in either 1911 or 1912; of course it was only a silent cinema'. [He then pointed to the rear wall] 'We found an artificial wall, which when removed revealed the original plaster screen. It was a bit dirty from all the years but there was a black frame all the way round it. In the bottom corner we found the signature of the man from Lyme Regis, who had plastered it.' [Regarding the lovely plaster work on the ceiling and upper walls] 'Oh yes it's all original, but actually it's not plaster it's papier mâché'. Then Mr Knight spoke of the people involved with the cinema: ' A lady, whose name I have forgotten ...used to sit in the right hand corner playing the piano. Mr A.W. Ellis was the manager of the cinema

The Picture Palace, Sidmouth. I have been told that the lady leaning out of the window is Mrs Ellis.

Interior of the Sidmouth Picture Palace, showing the original plaster screen; this is the only one I have found in Devon.

and he also had a photographic shop in New Street. There is a photograph of his wife and child, I assume, looking out of one of the bay windows at the front... The building was not a purpose-built cinema. It was built about 1875, I found the date on a rafter way up in the roof, and I believe it was [i.e. had been] *a cake shop.... I remember a picture of a board showing a kissing race or something suspended up on the front.'* [A 1924 photograph of the cinema shows this board, which is advertising the 1922 film *The Kissing Cup Race* starring Violet Hopson and a newcomer Clive Brook.] [T 22.6.98]

The cinema was to close with the opening of the Grand Cinema in 1929, at the time of the advent of the 'talkies' [22.6.98]

The architect's drawing, c1935, showing the conversion to the present shop premises.

46

The Cinema, Tavistock, a typical conversion of a building to use as a cinema as this new form of entertainment became popular.

Tavistock Cinemas: 1895 - 1914

Walford's Cinema Palace   Cornmarket, West Street 1912 - ??   FE

This cinema, like so many at the beginning of the century, was not purpose-built, but made use of existing premises, in this instance part of the Corn Market. It appears in KD for 1914 when the proprietor was Mr C. Walford. Mr Walford was running other cinemas in the county at this period, one has already been noted in Dawlish. By 1923 the owner is given as Mr A.S. Davis. It seems to have been a very popular place of entertainment, only closing its doors with the coming of a purpose-built cinema on Plymouth Road. [21.9.96]

Teignmouth Cinemas: 1895 - 1914

Riviera Cinema   The Den   c1910 - 2000

This building, which was still a working cinema until February 2000, has had a most interesting and, one might say, chequered career. It is doubtful if the original owners could ever have envisaged the uses to which their daydream

The Riviera Cinema, Teignmouth, as it looked in recent years until it closed in 2000.

The original building, shown here in its role as a restaurant, before becoming a picture palace.

Teignmouth, Bowling Green and Den Crescent.

of culture for the social élite of Teignmouth would be put. For the following outline of the building's history I am very much indebted to the present owner, Mr Peter Prince, whose father bought the property in 1924, for allowing me to quote fully from his own researches into the story of the Riviera Cinema:

'Built in 1826 by Lord Courtenay, plus forty shareholders, it had a ballroom 63 feet long. In 1830 it was leased for 60 years to the Teignmouth and East Devon Club. Then in 1890 it was actually sold to the club.

It became commercial in 1908 when a Mr Charles Sayce bought it for a restaurant. In 1912 Mr Charlie Poole leased the ballroom as a cinema. Safety regulations meant that the cinema was reached by two iron staircases and the projection box was added to the exterior. In 1924 Mr Bill Prince bought both the cinema and the restaurant for £2,500. In 1934 Mr Prince converted to a 'Super' at a cost of £33,000 ...[he did this in an attempt to stop any of the big circuits from opening a 'Super Cinema' in the town - in this he was successful.] The building was gutted and the veranda removed from the front. There was seating for 900. The 'new' Riviera

The Riviera, when the cinema was housed in the Ballroom, circa 1924.

The Riviera with the cinema now confined to the former balcony, following the conversion of the stalls area into an amusement arcade in 1970.

opened on 16th July 1934 with Jack Hulbert in 'Jack Ahoy'. In 1970 [as a result of falling numbers] *an amusement arcade replaced the stalls, and the balcony was enlarged to form the new cinema.*

It says a great deal for the care with which this conversion was carried out, that the cinema as I saw it gave no impression of having been truncated. One got the feeling of stepping back into a 1930s cinema in the golden days of the movies. In 1990 Mr Peter Hoare acquired the lease of the cinema, which he ran, together with the Radway at Sidmouth, the Savoy at Exmouth, the Alexandra at Newton Abbot, plus two other cinemas outside the county. Talking to Mr Hoare, and indeed to other owner/managers, one gets a very strong impression that running a cinema is for them a question of love first and money second. In at least one case brought to my attention, the owner was actually subsidising the cinema, to the annoyance of his accountant, from his other business. Sadly, the Riviera closed early in 2000 and its future is at present uncertain.

An early advertisement in the local newspaper tells us that the great French actress Sarah Bernhardt appeared here in her great film triumph *Queen Elizabeth* [1912]. It was the importation of this film, along with Italian epics such as *Quo Vadis* and *Cabiria*, to America that helped to boost the idea of the longer story film at a time when short, ten minute actualities were the norm. [2.10.96]

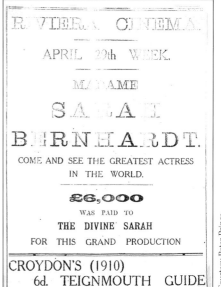

RIVIERA CINEMA.

APRIL 29th WEEK.

MADAME

SARAH

BERNHARDT.

COME AND SEE THE GREATEST ACTRESS IN THE WORLD.

£6,000

WAS PAID TO

THE DIVINE SARAH

FOR THIS GRAND PRODUCTION

CROYDON'S (1910)

6d. TEIGNMOUTH GUIDE

Sarah Bernhardt at The Riviera Cinema c1912.

Tiverton Cinemas: 1895 - 1914

Tiverton Electric Theatre   Newport Street   c1912 - c1970   BE

The Tiverton Electric Palace, which stands in Newport Street, was opened prior to 1914 and, happily, the building still stands, though it is now a bingo and snooker hall. In 1914 the KYB gives the owner as A.O. Ellis and the seating capacity as 800. It is typical of the period in having a grand façade but is far less imposing if seen from the rear. This, it must be said, was to remain true of much cinema architecture through to the Second World War. The manager in 1914 was Mr Percy Knott. However, by 1919, most likely as a result of the manpower shortage caused by the war, a Miss D. Potter was managing the cinema and was still doing so in 1923. By 1935 the position was

The Electric Cinema, Tiverton, showing a rather unusual layout to the façade.

A view of the rear of the Electric, typical of the less imposing auditorium section of many cinemas.

Littlewoods, Torquay, site of the former cinema Electric/ Colony, which opened in 1911 and only closed in 1986

held by Mrs. W.J. Varcoe. At the outbreak of the Second World War in 1939, the managership was again in male hands, in the person of Mr. W.E. Jones. Cinema managers played a crucial role in the history of cinema throughout the county. It is to them that many towns and even villages owe their share of movie magic over the years. They really worked to make their "kinema" a focus for entertainment in their own particular corner of Devon. We shall hear more of them later. The cinema survived until some time in the 1970s. In the 1969 Year Book the proprietor is given as L.G. Vearnacombe. The seating capacity had dropped from the original 800 to 398 seats. Cinemascope had been installed, it had continuous performances through the week, with matinées on Saturdays, and prices ranged from 2/6d to 5/-. When the Electric closed, this left the town's cinema entertainment in the hands, or seats, of the Tivoli Cinema, of which more at the appropriate time. [1.11.96]

Torquay Cinemas 1895 - 1914

Torquay Picturedrome   Market Street   1909 - 1935   [?]

The only Torquay cinema to appear in KD for this period is the Torquay Picturedrome in Market Street, with Mr William Mellor shown as proprietor. It would seem that this was a very early cinema, which I understand began life in part of Torquay Market, opening in September 1909. There was an update and general improvement to the cinema in 1913. In the 1914 KYB the owner is as given in KD, with the additional information that the cinema had a seating capacity of 1000. It operated from 1909 to 1935. The coming of the more opulent cinemas was probably the cause of its demise.

Electric / Colony   Union Street / Temperance Street 1911 - 1986   D

This was another early Torquay cinema which opened in 1911 and was in operation until 1986. This cinema is mentioned in the KYB of 1914 and 1917. This seems to have been the first purpose-built cinema in the town, costing £7,300, with seating for about 700 patrons. In October 1929 the Electric, as it was still called, was wired for the "talkies". A short time later, a balcony was added, thereby increasing the capacity of the cinema at a time of growing attendances. The building was demolished in the 1980s and Littlewoods now stands on or near the site. For many years it was owned and run by the late Mr Peter Myott. A short article in the 'Herald Express' (3. 5. 96) tells us that Mr Myott's widow, Mrs Eileen Myott, was to unveil a plaque at the Littlewood's Store to honour Mr Myott and the cinema that had stood on the site for 75 years. This is something of a rarity; most cinemas that fall to make way for redevelopment disappear without trace. I am happy to say that the plaque, and a very tasteful one at that, is now there for all to see.
[6.6.96] S [13.6.2000]S.

Plaque to mark the site of the Electric/Colony.

Empire / Cinedrome   Victoria Road 1913 - 1959 (1962 - 1963)   BE

The Empire, Victoria Road, was first built and owned by a Mr R. Tucker. However, by 1915 it was leased by Mr Charlie Poole. In the period 1916 to 1920 it went by the name of Cinedrome, yet another trap set for the unwary cinema researcher in later days.

It is said to be the first cinema in the town to install sound for the new "Talkies" and opened the sound era with *Broadway Melody* starring Charles King and Anita Page. The cinema was later sold to Mr W. Farrant Gilley, the owner of the Paignton Picture House and the Burlington. The Empire closed in 1959 with a short re-opening in 1962 / 63. It then became a venue for bingo and later still a night club. It suffered a fire in the projection area at some period in its history, but I have been unable, so far, to find a date for this event.

Fire! But the audience did not know

WHAT might have proved a serious fire, in the Empire Cinema, on Wednesday night, was averted by the presence of mind of Dennis Wollacott, 25-year-old projectionist, now living at Alexandra Road, Torquay.

At a few minutes past ten, shortly before the programme ended, he saw smoke and flames coming from a pile of films in the rewinding room. He threw sand and water on to the outbreak, and then, half suffocated, slammed the fireproof doors of the room and ran downstairs to telephone the Fire Brigade.

...the scene, and the fire was subdued within a quarter of an hour. Unfortunately, during fire-fighting operations an explosion occurred as a result of which four members of the brigade were caught in a flash of flame and received severe injuries to the face and hands. They were Company Officer William Potter, Section Leader Reginald Elson, Leading Fireman Arthur Pyne and Fireman Rupert Micholmore. They were rushed to Torbay Hospital, but after treatment were allowed to go home.

NO DANGER TO PATRONS

Divisional Officer D. W. Potts told the "Torquay Times" yesterday that it was largely due to the conduct of Mr. Wollacott and the effective fire prevention measures at the cinema, that more serious consequences were averted...

Fire in the box, a not uncommon hazard in the days of nitrate stock.

Empire, Torquay, with a very appropriate new name.

Despite the Great War, cinema continued to gain ground as the newest form of visual entertainment. It was a cheap form of entertainment that required no previous knowledge of earlier art forms. It appealed initially to the working classes, but with the advent of longer and more intellectual films, the middle classes were now beginning to take a serious interest in the movies. New and better picture houses were springing up in the more affluent areas of towns and cities, and these provided another means of drawing the middle classes into this new cinema craze. The above map does not tell the whole story: there were many travelling cinema shows also in operation at this time. The story of Braunton's cinema history illustrates this very well. Though not shown on the map, Braunton was not without its picture show at this period. (The details of Braunton's history are covered fully in the text).

DEVON CINEMAS
1814 - 1919

The period from 1914 to 1919, which covers the time of the Great War, was a traumatic period not only for the country itself, and indeed the whole of Europe, but also for the film industries within those countries. Until 1914, no single country had the lead on any other in film production nor in the growing industry of exhibition. Until the outbreak of war, film production in Europe was on a par with that in the United States. In fact, in terms of originality and quality, European cinema had the edge. The outbreak of war in Europe was to change all that. By the time peace returned to Europe, the United States dominated the world film industry and has done so ever since. (For an excellent account of this take-over, see David Puttnam's *The Undeclared War*.} By 1918 approximately 80% of the world's films were coming from what would soon be known as the Hollywood Film Factory. In Europe during the war years, the production side of the industry suffered from a chronic lack of raw materials; by the time peace was restored, the United States had a stranglehold on the business of film production which it has never relinquished.

WW1. 'The World is Mine'. Typical of the period.

DAILY ROUTINE OF A SOLDIER'S LIFE TOLD IN HYMNS.

6.30 a.m.	Reveille	Christains awake.
6.45 ,,	Hut Parade	Art thou weary.
7. 0 ,,	Breakfast	Meekly wait and murmur not.
8.15 ,,	C.O.'s Parade	When he cometh.
8.45 ,,	Manœuvres	Fight the good fight.
9.30 ,,	Company Order	Oft in danger, oft in woe.
10.30 ,,	Kit Inspection	All things bright and beautiful.
11.15 ,,	Sweedish drill	Here we suffer grief and pain
1. 0 p.m.	Dinner	Come, ye thankful people, come.
2.15 ,,	Rifle Drill	Go labour on.
4.15 ,,	Dismiss	Praise God from whom all blessings flow
5. 0 ,,	Tea	What means this eager anxious throng.
6. 0 ,,	Free for the night	O, Lord, how happy should we be.
6.30 ,,	Officer's Lecture	Tell me the old, old story.
10. 0 ,,	Last Post	All are safely gathered in.
10.15 ,,	Lights out	Peace, perfect peace.
10.30 ,,	Inspection Guards	Sleep on, beloved.
	Night Manœuvres	Lead kindly light.
	Zeppelin Raids	We plough the fields and scatter, A. MEN.

WW1 Daily Routine: postcard.

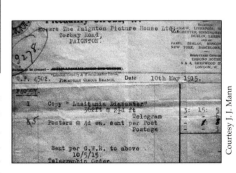

WW1 Sinking of the Lusitania, film receipt dated 10. 5. 1915. Lusitania only sank on the 7. 5.1915. Quick work by somebody !

But while film-making declined in Britain and the rest of Europe, audiences flocked in ever greater numbers to the picture houses. But even here there was a major problem, and that was lack of manpower to run the cinemas. The rush of men volunteering for the armed forces in the early part of the war was then followed by conscription. This drain on manpower covered the whole spectrum of employment and the cinema industry was no exception. Many cinemas were forced to close, usually with no hope of re-opening later. In some cases women took over the jobs left vacant by conscription. This was not always possible and indeed at this period the idea of women taking on men's

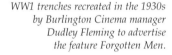
ADMIRAL JELLICOE.

WW1: Admiral Jellicoe, a grand naval hero.

jobs was frowned upon. It is true that women had acted as cashiers and usherettes from the early days, but now they were taking over not only as projectionists but even in some cases as managers. This aspect is well covered in Audrey Field's most entertaining and informative book *Picture Palace* (Gentry Books - London - 1974). Though none of her examples is taken from Devon, the pattern was nationwide and must in some cases have applied here. For evidence, we note the history of managership at the Tiverton Electric Theatre mentioned above. There was not the loss of cinemas, through bombing, that occurred in the later conflict but one doubts whether money, manpower or materials were available to keep up with decoration, maintenance or repairs.

The role played by cinemas in the Great War was very similar to that which they played a generation later. They provided both civilians and servicemen and women with a cheap means of forgetting, for a couple of hours, the war with all its tragedies, separations and heartbreaks. Even in this early conflict, both sides saw the need for boosting morale and both sides turned to the cinema to do just that. The great American director D.W. Griffith was brought to this country, at the express invitation of the government, to make a morale-boosting film. He was given *carte blanche* to make the film and was even allowed, with his stars Lillian and Dorothy Gish, to visit and film at the front. It may be of passing interest that a very young Noël Coward appeared briefly in this epic, *Hearts of the World*, which was made in 1917. It is against this background that the rest of this section must be seen.

By the end of 1914, using the figures provided by KD, there were 31 cinemas in 17 towns in Devon. By the end of 1919 there were 42 cinemas in 23 towns. There are similar figures in the KYB. Given the restrictions imposed by the Great War, this increase of approximately 26% is quite impressive. It shows that even during the greatest armed conflict ever to darken the history of the world, cinema was seen by the ordinary men and women as a vital part of their lives. No nation saw fit to close its cinemas, and in fact governments on both sides of the Atlantic realised that, in cinema, they had the most powerful tool for forming opinions and boosting morale that the world had ever seen. This is no idle speculation as the following quotation proves:

"Precisely because of the powerful political and military influence that film will continue to wield for the duration of the war, our victory absolutely depends on

WW1 trenches recreated in the 1930s by Burlington Cinema manager Dudley Fleming to advertise the feature Forgotten Men.

our using films to exert the greatest possible persuasion wherever people can still be won over to the German cause."

(Ludendorff: Memo to Prussian war minister - July 1917)

We will see this same attitude expressed, in much the same words, during the rise of Nazism in the 1930s and throughout the Second World War. Again, all nations saw film as a critical part of their war effort. It should be noted, however, that films made during the Second World War were far more subtle and less hysterical than those made during the earlier conflict.

Some Important Films produced 1914 - 1919

Birth of a Nation (US)	*1915*	*D.W. Griffith*
Intolerance (US)	*1916*	*D.W. Griffith*
Easy Street (US)	*1917*	*Charlie Chaplin*
Shoulder Arms (US)	*1917*	*Charlie Chaplin*
Hearts of the World (US)	*1918*	*D.W. Griffith*
Cabinet of Dr. Caligari (Germany)	*1919*	*Robert Wiene*

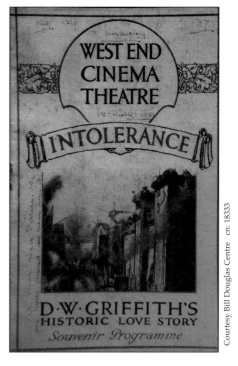

Intolerance, Griffith's greatest epic.

Lillian Gish, the greatest of Griffith's actresses.

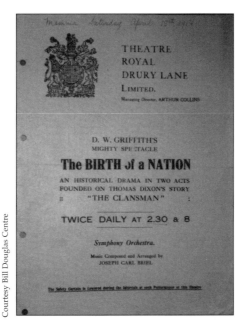

Birth of a Nation. The first of Griffith's masterpieces.

Hearts of the World: with Lillian & Dorothy Gish.

Barnstaple Cinemas: 1914 - 1919

Foresters Hall Picture Palace   Bear Street?   1919 - c1930s [?]

This cinema opened in February 1919 as a model of the up-to-date picture house. There was one show daily, commencing at eight o'clock. I suspect, given the name, that this was in fact a multi-use venue. There seems to be some confusion over the address of this cinema. A history of Barnstaple, *Barnstaple: A Town on the Taw,* gives the address in Bear Street, as shown above. However, in KD for 1919, the address is given as High Street, but in the 1923 edition of that publication the address is given as 2, Silver Street. The proprietor for both 1919 and 1923 is given as Albany Ward, who owned or ran many

The Palladium, Bideford, which opened in 1919. This was, I understand, the main entrance.

The Palladium, Bideford: the rear of the cinema, which is only yards from the old Bijou Cinema.

cinemas in the south-west. The cinema does not appear in the 1935 directory and so I assume that it closed some time between 1923 and 1935.

Bideford Cinemas: 1914 - 1919

Palladium Cinema   Mill Street 1919 - 1926   BE

The Palladium opened just after the Great War: the building remains to this day but the cinema itself closed in 1926. Unfortunately, there seems to be very little left of the interior to give a clue to its former use. This cinema, like the Bijou, ran live shows as well as showing films. This was a practice that went on in some cinemas for many years. The Granada cinema chain was still doing this in the 1950s. [16.7.97]

Bovey Tracey: 1914 - 1919

Bovey Tracey Town Hall   c1914 - c1950s   BE

Cinema started fairly early in Bovey Tracey. The KYB for 1917 states that the Town Hall was showing films at that date: there is no indication of the owner / lessee or any other details. Films continued to be shown there until after the Second World War. The cinema was actually above the fire station. When I talked about Devon cinemas on Radio Devon early in 1998, one gentleman telephoned in to say that he had been a regular patron. He went on to say that, when the fire engine was called out, it was impossible to hear the sound track. But there was never any question of getting your money back when this happened. However, it was not the noise of the fire-engine that actually emptied the cinema on one occasion, it was the rush of patrons to see the burning down of the local chip shop.   [2.10.96]

Town Hall Cinema, Bovey Tracey, situated above the Fire Station, and could be very noisy.

Brixham Town Hall ?? BE

Brixham Town Hall was an early venue for visual entertainment in Brixham. Paul's Myorama was playing here in 1906. At around the same date, a film called *Trip to the Moon* was shown. This would appear to be the Georges Méliès film (1902), now considered one of the great classics of early cinema.

Town Hall Cinema, Brixham. A very imposing building in which films were shown from as early as 1906.

The Electric, Brixham, showing the present rather plain façade, but happily well cared for.

Electric **Fore Street c1914 - ??** **[?]**

The Electric appears in the 1914 and 1917 editions of KYB and then appears in KD from 1923 to 1939. KYB gives the proprietor in 1914 & 1917 as A.O. Ellis. KD in 1923 gives Miss J. Dunford as manageress, while in 1935 & 1939 the managing director is E.O. Ellis. It must be noted here that another source states that the Electric Cinema was built in Fore Street, opened in 1935 and closed in 1966. This cinema was built by the firm of Cooksley and the architect was W. Moxhay of St. Marychurch. I am left wondering if there were two cinemas of this name in Brixham or whether the second was merely a rebuilding of the first. See entry for the Regent in the next section.

Dartmouth Cinemas: 1914 - 1919

Cinedrome / Palladium **Anzac Street :c1919 - c1923 [1950s?]** **BE**

This cinema, formerly the Palladium Electric Theatre in Hanover Street, appears in the 1919 edition of KD but then disappears. However, by 1923 the

The rear view of the Electric, Brixham. One wonders how much this view has changed since it closed in 1966.

Dartmouth Picture House appears in the same street. I am assuming that these two are one and the same, with both the cinema and the street changing names. This was a very common practice, as many other examples in this study illustrate. Sometimes it occurred with a change of ownership, sometimes for no apparent reason. The change of street name is less common, though it occurred in Okehampton, for example, when Market Street became Lodge Road on a 1923 O/S map. It has now reverted to the original name. The site of the Dartmouth Palladium is now occupied by a shopping arcade. The name Palladium remains above the Anzac Street entrance, with a short notice stating that the conversion was made in 1987 by local builders. [7.5.98]

Dawlish Cinemas: 1914 - 1919

Walfords Cinema   Chapel Street c1914 - ?   [?]

Walfords Cinema in Chapel Street, KD 1914, does not appear in the 1919 edition so one might suppose that this cinema closed during this period, although there seems to be some doubt regarding the fate or even the existence of this cinema. There is no mention of any cinema in Dawlish at this period in the KYB, but see earlier Dawlish entry.

Devonport Cinemas: 1914 - 1919

Ford Palladium   St Levan Road, Ford   c1916 - 1964   BE

The Ford Palladium opened during the Great War and the building survives to this day despite the blitz, and a fire in more recent years. It was a single storey building, long and narrow, but with a certain distinction that is still evident today. It is now a builders' merchant but such has been the careful rebuilding of the exterior that it is still possible to see, as I did when I visited the site in 1997, what eager cinema patrons would have seen as they made their way to the 'flicks' in the heyday of cinema going. This early cinema, unlike many later purpose-built cinemas, fits in well with its surroundings. [25.6.97]

The Ford Palladium, Plymouth, Despite the blitz, and a later fire, the building is still recognisable as the cinema it once was.

Rear and side view of the Palladium, showing a long narrow building, which was not unusual in cinemas of this period.

EXETER CINEMAS: 1914 - 1919

Exeter saw no new cinemas during this period, but it lost the Victoria Hall, which was burnt down in 1919. Plans were drawn up to rebuild this multi-use hall but in fact no actual building resulted.

GREAT TORRINGTON CINEMAS: 1914 - 1919

The Cinema   Church Lane   pre 1919 - ??   BE

When I visited Great Torrington in 1997 I found this seemingly small cinema tucked away and practically lost and forgotten. It had, at some point, been converted to bingo. At this time it displayed a 'For Sale' notice on its sadly shabby façade. This façade was very small and cramped, and it was surprising to find, on walking around the side, just how far back this building went. The rear wall was covered in greenery and I declined the kind offer of the man who lived next door, to borrow his ladder to explore the roof. There are limits to what one will undertake in the name of research! [16.7.97]

The Cinema, Great Torrington. A very simple façade looking very unloved when I visited in 1997.

The Cinema, Great Torrington. The small façade hides a much larger auditorium than one might expect.

Ilfracombe Cinemas: 1914 - 1919

The Picture Hall   Northfield Street   1915 - 1916 [1951]   BE

In 1915 the Picture Hall in Northfield Street changed its name to the Electric Theatre. In 1916 this changed again when the Electric Theatre became the Empire Theatre. All the time it remained on the upper floor of the Rechabite Hall. There were to be two more name changes before this cinema closed on 1st October 1951.[17.7.97]

Okehampton Cinemas 1915 - 1919

Picture Palace / Premier   Market Street   1915 - 1960s   BE

Author's collection

The Picture Palace/Premier, Okehampton

The Okehampton Picture Palace, as it was originally known, opened in 1915. The building had previously been used by Cornish, a firm of drapers, and the conversion was undertaken by Blatchford and Dawe. The cinema appears in KD for 1923 and again in 1935, when the address is given as Lodge Road. At first I thought that there had been two cinemas of that name in Okehampton; however, help was on hand from the museum staff, who located a map of the period (1923) in which Market Street was shown as Lodge Road. The 1939 edition of KD shows that by this time the cinema had been renamed the Premier, though some suggest that the name change came earlier with the advent of the 'talkies' circa 1929/30. The 1935 KYB gives the seating as 300, but no other details. The 1963 KYB gives the owner as A.M. Newcombe, whereas the 1939 KD gives Simon Newcombe as the proprietor. As the cinema does not appear in the 1969 edition of the KYB, I assume that the Premier ceased, as a picture palace, sometime between 1963 and 1969. A photograph of the staff in 1925 shows the commissionaire and the chocolate boy in full uniform. Also in the picture are the projectionist and the cinema pianist. The Premier, along with so many other cinemas, great and small, was forced to close when other forms of mass entertainment, including television, became popular in the post-war years. For a time it functioned as a supermarket and then became a night-club called Nero's, which it still was when I re-visited Okehampton in 1998. [2.9.97]

Ottery St. Mary Cinemas: 1914 - 1919

The Palace / Scala   6 Jesu Street   Pre 1919 - c1950s   BE

This small cinema opened sometime between 1914 and 1919. It continued in service until the fall in attendances made it uneconomic in the 1950s/60s. It appears for the first time in the 1919 edition of KD as The Palace. In the 1935 edition of KD it has been renamed the Scala. Nothing now shows on the exterior to give any indication that this was once a thriving cinema. I would quote from a letter I received early in 1998, which describes the pleasures of cinema-going at the Scala in 'younger and happier days' :

"Yes I remember the Scala very well. The very first film I saw there was Laurel & Hardy Meet the Ghosts [I can find no film of that name in the Laurel & Hardy canon, but would suggest that it might be their 1942 feature A-Haunting We Will Go] - it gave me nightmares !! The cinema was run by a single family (can't remember the name) - Dad was the projectionist, Mum sold the tickets and the daughter - if she had finished her homework - tore them up again and showed you to your seat. In those days we had Movietone News, which was only a few weeks old ! The roof was galvanised iron - OK if it only rained, but if it hailed you couldn't hear the sound track. If the film wasn't too popular, the first six people were allowed in

free - if nobody else arrived they were sent home, but if more did come, Mum came round to collect your money! Happy memories."

Mr David Townsend via Roger Free - Rattery

Today it appears as one of a small terrace in Jesu Street, now functioning as retail premises. However, from inside it is possible to see something of its former glory. Plaster on the walls of what was once the auditorium gives some clue, as does the former projection box, which appears to be set at the side rather than on the centre line of the auditorium. [14.5.96]

The Scala, Ottery St Mary. Interior gives the game away, note projection box and décor.

The Scala, Ottery St. Mary. A very hidden cinema.

Paignton Cinemas: 1914 - 1919

Triangle Cinedrome   Totnes Road   pre 1919 - c1960s   BE

This cinema seems to have changed its name to the Electric Palace some time before 1923 when it was in the hands of Major A.O. Ellis, who remained the owner until circa 1939. In that year the manageress was a Miss M. Howard. It had closed by 1969. One of the reasons for the closure was that the queues forming in the then narrow road, which at that time had two way traffic, caused major problems. This information comes from Mr J.J. Mann, the last manager of the Torbay Cinema; at the period under discussion both cinemas were under the same management, Paignton Picture Houses Ltd. [21.2.98]

Plymouth Cinemas: 1914 - 1919

Electric Theatre   St. John's Road 1914 - c1930   [?]

I had found little information on this cinema until Pat Ghillyer came to the rescue. The Electric appears in KD for 1919 and 1923 and the KYB for 1914 and 1917, but has gone from the KD by 1935. Pat Ghillyer gives a closing date of late 1930s, as well as the following outline history of the Electric. The cinema opened in 1914 on the first floor of what had been a factory. It was known locally, as indeed were many small venues, as The Bughouse. An early, possibly the first film shown, was *The Life of Christ.* (Gaumont - France - 1906. It was directed by Alice Guy: she was one of the very first female directors, and should be honoured as such.) It seems that part of the building was used as a dance hall and the noise filtered through to the cinema, which must have been

The Triangle/ Electric Picturedrome, Paignton.

something of a distraction to the patrons trying to watch the film. There is a suggestion that the building was later used both as a youth club and then by the army.

Picture House   **George Street   1919 - 1922**   **Bz**

According to Plymouth Cinema historian, Pat Ghillyer, this was a cinema with a very short life. It was built on a site formerly used by Spearman the drapers. After the cinema closed, the site was used, from 1923 to 1940, by Burton's the tailors. Another Plymouth cinema, the Criterion Kinema, also went over to the clothing trade when it closed in 1939, before suffering in the blitz.

Plympton St. Mary Cinemas: 1914 -1919

The Cinema   **Ridgeway   pre 1919 - ??**   **[?]**

This cinema appears in the 1919 edition of KD and again in 1923 but has gone by the 1935 edition. This may well be one of those cinemas that was forced to close with the coming of sound after 1927. I have been unable to find any picture of this cinema.

Seaton Cinemas: 1914 - 1919

The Town Hall Cinema   **Town Hall   Pre 1919 - c 1935   BE**

This cinema, situated in the Town Hall, was one of a number of cinemas that used existing premises to show films. I have been unable to discover whether it showed films on a full-time or part-time basis but I suspect the latter. It appears in the 1919 edition of KD and again in 1923; it does not appear in the 1935 edition but the Regal Cinema does. This would suggest that the opening of the Regal forced this earlier cinema to close. This was a very common occurrence, a pattern which recurred in the 1990s with the building of the multiplex cinemas. [27.10.97]

Seaton, The Town Hall Cinema. Such public buildings were often the first home of the movies in many towns.

Author's collection

Courtesy Tony Moss

Site of the former Lyceum Cinema.
Teignmouth.

Teignmouth Cinemas 1914 - 1919.

Lyceum Cinema **Somerset Place Pre 1919 - ???** **[?]**

The Lyceum opened prior to 1919 and then appears in the 1923 , 1935 and 1939 editions of KD. In the 1917 edition of the KYB, the owner is given as Clayton (sic). It was only as this book was going to press that a picture of the cinema came into my hands, and that only after it had ceased to function as a cinema. It seems to have survived the Second World War and to have gone on into the (?)1950s. In both the 1914 and 1917 edition of the KYB the Assembly Rooms are shown, which must refer to the cinema now known as the Riviera. For details of this cinema see the Riviera entry.

Torquay Cinemas: 1914 - 1919

Torquay Picturedrome **Market Street 1909 - 1935** **[?]**

Formerly known as the **Market Hall Cinema,** as noted in section one, this early cinema seems to have been yet another cinema that found itself unable to meet the competition of the larger, more opulent picture houses that made their appearance in the 1930s. I have included it again here as, under the name Torquay Picturedrome, it appears in the 1919, 1923 and 1935 edition of KD. It appears in both the 1914 and 1917 edition of the KYB. Here the owner is noted as L.W. Mellor. The seating capacity is given as 1000, which seems high for a town of this size at that date, but speaks volumes for the hold cinema already had on audiences world-wide.

By 1922 we can almost see the pattern of cinema distribution in its final form. The weighting to the south of the country is clearly marked, with the holiday centres being the favoured venues for this newest form of visual entertainment. As might be expected, it was Plymouth (by far the largest centre of population in the county) that had the greatest concentration of picture palaces. The large cinema chains had yet to make their mark, and it was still the local cinema, often owned and run by a local family, which provided large areas of the county with their diet of Hollywood Dreams

DEVON CINEMAS
1920 - 1923

Although a short period, this is an important one in that it saw the growth and development of the cinema circuits. Circuits had begun to form prior to the Great War and most of these were in the provinces. By the war year of 1917, there were 90 circuits in Britain with a total of 429 cinemas.* Just over a quarter of these, approximately 114, were owned by just 8 circuits. The rest were owned by smaller circuits with an average of 4 cinemas each. The largest of these circuits was Albany Ward, based in Weymouth, with 28 cinemas in the south-west. As early as 1914 we note that the Palladium in Exeter was owned by Albany Ward. By 1919 he was also running the Foresters Hall Picture House in Barnstaple. The pattern by 1920 was very much as in 1917 with an increase both in circuits and the actual number of cinemas. However, the largest of the circuits by this date was The Provincial Cinematograph Theatres, a national circuit based in London, with 33 cinemas. By 1926 this figure had risen to 75. This circuit (PCT) was later to take over the Albany Ward circuit. It should be noted that in 1928 the PCT was itself acquired by the Gaumont-British Picture Corporation which by 1930 had 200 cinemas in its control. At this date the other 'giant' group was Maxwell's ABC circuit with 118 cinemas.

* (*Figures taken from* The History of the British Cinema - *Rachael Low 1971.*)

By this time film stars were really coming into their own. They had been mere faces for a while, but soon their drawing power at the box office made them aware of their value to the studios. Their power base was shattered with the coming of sound.

Author's collection

If the country as a whole was suffering from the ravages of four years of war, the cinema exhibition industry was booming. This was not true of production. As noted above, by 1918 approximately 80% of films shown in British cinemas, and indeed world cinemas, came from The United States. The list given below bears this out. It should be noted that the German industry was making great strides, as was production in Sweden. However, all the European directors whose works are listed below were later to be found in Hollywood, along with stars like Greta Garbo, Lars Hanson and Marlene Dietrich.

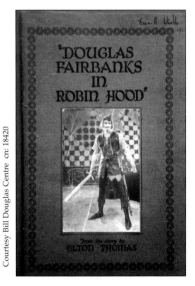

Four Horsemen of the Apocalypse: Palladium, Exeter.

The Covered Wagon, 1923. The Western was always a popular subject for Hollywood, as it depicted America's own recent mythic history.

Fairbanks' Robin Hood, 1923, is typical of his swash-buckling period, but not one of his best.

Important Films in circulation between 1920 and 1923:

Title	Director	Starring
Anne Boleyn (1920)	*Ernst Lubitch (G)*	*Emil Jannings*
Way Down East (1920)	*D.W. Griffith (US)*	*Lillian Gish*
		Richard Barthelmess
Nanook of the North (1920)	*Robert Flaherty (US)*	*(Documentary)*
Four Horsemen of the Apocalypse (1920)	*Rex Ingram (US)*	*Rudolph Valentino*
Tol'able David (1921)	*Henry King (US)*	*Richard Barthlemess*
Nosfaratu (Dracula) (1922)	*F.W. Murnau (G)*	*Max Schreck*
Robin Hood (1923)	*Alan Dwan (US)*	*Fairbanks Snr*
Safety Last (1923)	*Sam Taylor (US)*	*Harold Lloyd*
The Covered Wagon (1923)	*James Cruze (US)*	*Ernest Torrence*
		Lois Wilson
Woman of Paris (1923)	*Charles Chaplin (US)*	*Adolphe Menjou*
Greed (1923)	*Eric von Stroheim (US)*	*Zasu Pitts*
Atonement of Gosta Berling (1923)	*Mauritz Stiller (Sw)*	*Greta Garbo,*
		Lars Hanson

The above list makes clear that by this date Hollywood, for most US films were now produced there rather than on the east coast, was making films in most of the classic genres. We see examples of the drama, melodrama, comedy, western, swashbuckler and anti-war film. The musical is absent in this still silent period, though silent versions of operas and operettas were made, for example Eric von Stroheim's 1925 version of *The Merry Widow* and the 1915 C. B. De Mille silent *Carmen*, starring the Metropolitan Opera singer Geraldine Farrar.

Appledore Cinemas:

The Gaiety   109 Irsha Street   c1920s - c1950s   BE

I found this charming little cinema in July 1997 when researching in North Devon. The building appears to have begun life in 1893, possibly as a Methodist chapel: the date is carved on the façade over the main door. It became a cinema between 1919 and 1923, though I have yet to find the exact date, and continued though to the 1950s. At present it is a private residence and it was through the kindness of the current owners, Mr & Mrs Clarkson, that I was able to tour the whole building. The screen end, the part overlooking the estuary, had been converted into very desirable living quarters, and the centre section was used as an attic. Posters of the last film shown, the name board that once graced Irsha Street along with other memorabilia were to be found in this area. It is the section facing out onto Irsha Street that is the most exciting. On the ground floor, the foyer still contains the box office, complete with telephone and prices shown on the glass screen surrounding the pay box. Upstairs, the projection room is complete, with one of the two original projectors still in situ. The time that I spent here was, perhaps, the happiest time of the whole research programme. It cannot be too strongly emphasised that this whole building is private property, the home of Mr & Mrs Clarkson. [16.7.97]

Gaiety, Appledore, showing its very plain façade

Gaiety, Appledore, the projection box, left as if in use.

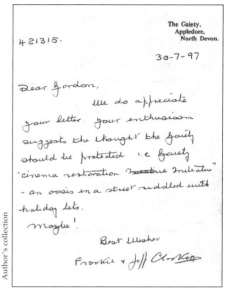

Gaiety: letter from the owners, Mr & Mrs Clarkson.

BRAUNTON CINEMAS: 1920 - 1923

The Cinema Caen Street c1920 - 1934 D

When I visited Braunton in July 1997 I was unable to trace this cinema. At that time, such information as I was able to glean led me to assume that it was a small local cinema, run by Sidney Tiller, which closed with the opening of the larger Plaza Cinema on Exeter Road in 1935. As I was in the final stages of writing this book, more information came to hand: Mr. V Thompson put me in touch with Mrs Anne Elliot, whose father, Mr Frank Farrar, had been both cinema pianist and manager of a cinema in Braunton. The story of Braunton's cinemas is fascinating and also typical of the way cinema became such a central part of people's lives in the first half of this century.

Braunton's cinema history: manager's business card.

The site of the first cinema in Braunton was in Perryman's Field, now part of the Caen Field Shopping Precinct. It was a mobile unit mounted on a lorry and it showed silent black and white films once a week. There was no pianist at this stage and the seating consisted of wooden bench seats inside the lorry. The approximate dates for this venue are 1920 - 1926. The second venue chosen by Mr Tiller has also disappeared, this time under the Cross Tree Centre in Chaloners Road. The cinema is described as a long building with a tin roof, having seating on long wooden benches. The films were still silents, but by this time there were two shows weekly, on Wednesday and Saturday. The projectionist was on the same level as the audience. There is some dispute as to prices: one source gives 1d, another 2d. This cinema was in operation circa 1926 and closed when a local firm bought the land on which the cinema stood, and built a large garage. Following this set-back, the showing of films moved, for a short time, to the Ex-Serviceman's Hall, which was situated in the Agricultural Inn. Cinema venue number four was the Parish Hall in Chaloners Road. It was owned and run by Mr J.L Penny from c1926 to 1928. It was then bought by Mr S.E. Reynolds of the Empire Cinema, Ilfracombe. This purchase is confirmed in a letter to Mr Farrar, dated 10th February 1928. It was brief and to the point:

Braunton's cinema history: letter to Mr Farrar

AUDIBLE FILMCRAFT LIMITED

Directors:
GEORGE W. PEARSON *Chairman*

GEORGE BANFIELD
F. NORMAN'S HURST
ALDERMAN S. CRESSWELL
WALTER SCOTT
DAVID W. MARWICK
GEORGE L. JEREMIAH
ALDERMAN T. E. COWNS, J.P.

Registered Offices:
155, OXFORD STREET,
LONDON. W.1.

Studios:
ELSTREE
WORTON HALL
WALTHAMSTOW

Secretary:
HENRY F. TIERNEY

Branches:
BIRMINGHAM CARDIFF
GLASGOW LEEDS
LIVERPOOL MANCHESTER
NEWCASTLE BELFAST

In reply please quote SG1/MS.

21st. January 1931.

F. Farrar, Esq.,
Braunton Cinema,
Braunton.
Devon.

Dear Sir,

We have your letter of yesterday's
date and note that the hall has now been taken
over by Mr. Drake.

As requested we enclose account
showing amount outstanding up to date.

We are writing to our Cardiff
Branch to-day and will ask Mr. Ballard to call
on you.

Yours faithfully,
For AUDIBLE FILMCRAFT LIMITED,

Accounts Dept.

Braunton's cinema history:
Mr G. Drake takes over the cinema.

F. Farrar, Esq.,

Cinema,

Braunton. Devon.

TEAR AT ABOVE PERFORATION.

STATEMENT

TELEPHONE: REGENT 7504. TELEGRAMS: PROSCREEN, WESDO, LONDON.

155 OXFORD STREET,

I.1. LONDON, W.1. 21st Jan. 1931

ALSO AT BIRMINGHAM, CARDIFF, LEEDS, MANCHESTER,
NEWCASTLE, GLASGOW & BELFAST.

DR. TO ...

AUDIBLE FILMCRAFT LTD.

E. & O. E.
1930

						£		
Nov. 13-	Balance	News.		7629		£ -	8	9
Dec. 27.								
Nov.	14	Carr.	"	245. L.1988.			1	3
"	2	"	"	247.)				
Dec.,	25	"	"	248)				
"	10	"	"	249)	5558		5	3
"	12	"	"	250)				
Nov.	28	"	"	246	5571		1	4
Dec. 29 -								
Jan. 21st.News.				7755		1	6	3
						£ 2 2		10

If only these prices still applied.
Braunton Cinema

Dear Sir,

Re Cinema Business at Braunton Parish Hall

I am writing to inform you that Mr. S.E. Reynolds of Ilfracombe, Cinema Proprietor, has purchased the above business, formerly carried on by the late Mr J.L. Penny, including the machinery, plant and effects, and will take over as from and including tomorrow the 11th instant.

Yours faithfully,

T. Oerton Junr. (Solicitor)

Mr F. Farrar, 4 Caen Street, Braunton.

This brisk communication was preceded by a personal letter to Mr Farrrar from Mr Reynolds, dated 6th February, inviting Mr Farrar to an evening meeting the next day to *'discuss matters generally, your expenses will of course be met'*. This arrangement was short-lived. In January 1931 the cinema was purchased by Mr George Drake: Mr Frank Farrar remained the manager and also, even at this late date, the cinema pianist; though a letter and an invoice, both dated 21st January 1931, from 'Audible Filmcrafts Limited' would suggest that talkies were now forming at least part of the programme. I have before me a copy of the agreement between Mr George Drake [employer] and Mr Frank Farrar [manager] made in 1931. This is obviously a draft copy, without date or signatures, but it sets out clearly and simply the terms of employment. Shows were held twice weekly on Wednesday and Saturday, with a Saturday matinée. Prices are given as 3d or 6d, but for children the matinée was a ha'penny, and the films were black and white silents, with pianist. (The projectionist was now on the balcony.) This cinema continued for a few years until Mr Drake built and opened the Plaza Cinema in Exeter Road in 1934. This cinema, the Plaza, is covered in section four. Mr Frank Farrar, who had given much of his life to cinema in Braunton, died four years later in 1938, aged 42, leaving a widow and three children. I am greatly indebted to his youngest daughter, Mrs Anne Elliot, for providing me with the fruits of her own research into the history of Braunton's cinemas.

BRIXHAM CINEMAS: 1920 - 1923

The Regent   **Fore Street**   **c1923 - 1966**   **BE**

The Regent Cinema is shown (KD) in Fore Street in 1923 when the manager was Mr Robert Strickland. However, it does not appear in the 1935 edition of that directory but the Electric Theatre does appear in Fore Street. This is another example of a cinema changing its name, but in this case it soon reverted to its original name (Electric Theatre) and continued to operate under that name until it closed in 1966. In 1935 the managing director is shown as E.O. Ellis. This seems to have been a family business as, in the same year, A.W. Ellis is given as the proprietor of the Cinema Picture Palace in Sidmouth (1919, 1923) and later The Grand, Sidmouth in 1935, but by 1939 Mr. Charles F. Cheshire had become the proprietor. The founding father would appear to be A.O. Ellis who is given as proprietor of the Northfield Picture Palace, Ilfracombe from 1914 to 1923. Between 1923 and 1939 Major A.O. Ellis is given as proprietor of the Electric Palace, Paignton; also in 1923 as proprietor of the Picture House, Buckfastleigh, and in 1939 he was running the Electric Theatre, Devonport, in place of E.O. Ellis. This appears to have been a small family business, which fits the pattern of smaller circuits mentioned earlier, which at this period had an average of 4 cinemas in their control.

*Buckfastleigh, Picture House:
interior showing the balcony.*

Buckfastleigh Cinemas: 1920 - 1923

Picture House   Station Road   c1922 - 1964   D

When I visited the site of this former cinema (now a tiny car park) in July 1998,
I had been able to discover little about this small cinema though, as mentioned above, in 1923 Major A.O. Ellis was the proprietor. However, as a result
of this visit, I was able to contact the grandson (Mr Richard Pickles) of the
next owner, a Mr William Pickles. The Pickles family then ran the cinema until
it closed in 1960. In 1962 it re-opened under a different management but closed
again, this time finally, in 1964. The Pickles family had moved down from
Yorkshire at the end of the Great War. It appears that in 1929 the cinema closed
for a period and was then re-opened by Mr. William Pickles, who in time
was succeeded by his son Mr Ernest Pickles.   The cinema was damaged

*Buckfastleigh, Picture House: Mrs Pickles
and friend by the impressive entrance
to the cinema*

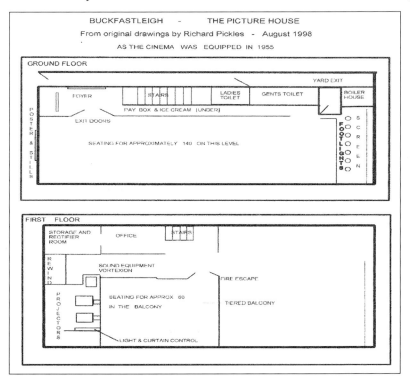

*Plan of the Picture House re-drawn
from sketch by Richard Pickles.*

by a fire during the Second World War, though not as the result of a visit from the Luftwaffe: a careless cigarette may have been the cause. It was rebuilt and it was at this time that a balcony was added. In 1955 CinemaScope was installed. The staff at this time consisted of a projectionist assisted by Mr Ernest Pickles. *"Mum* [Mrs Pickles] *and a lady called Pat manned the Pay Box and there was an usherette or two, plus a lad and me".* [R.P.] Mr Richard Pickles, who was a boy at the time, attributes the closure of the cinema to falling audience numbers plus the Entertainment Tax then in force.

The 1917 edition of the KYB names the Town Hall & Institution as the film venue for Buckfastleigh in earlier years and I have been told that after the cinema closed, films were shown in the function room of the King's Arms. [10.7.98]

Town Hall Cinema, Crediton

Courtesy Albert Labbett

Author's collection

Town Hall Cinema, Chulmleigh. Both rather imposing venues for the antics of Buster Keaton & Harold Lloyd.

Crediton Cinemas: 1920 ~ 1923

Town Hall Cinema   **High Street c1923 - c1931**   **BE**
This cinema was, like so many at the period, run by a family, in this case a local farming family along with a son-in-law, who was Headmaster of a local school. It was situated in a multi-purpose building, at a time when it did not seem economically viable to erect a purpose-built cinema. Many towns never actually had a purpose-built cinema of their own, and people either made do with what they had or went to the nearest town that had one. The Town Hall Cinema was to provide Crediton with its diet of Hollywood dreams until the **Palace Cinema** was opened in East Street in about 1931. This will be covered in the appropriate section. [4.12.96]

Dartmouth Cinemas: 1920 ~ 1923

Cinedrome Electric Theatre   Mayor's Avenue   c1920s - c1970   D
This would seem to be the first named cinema on this site. I have found out nothing of its early history. However the later Royalty / Maxime stood in Mayor's Avenue until demolished to make way for the new Health Centre in the 1970s. This was one of the chain of cinemas run after the Second World

War by Mr Charles (Charlie) Scott, who is most affectionately spoken of by all who knew him, especially Mr Peter Hoare who now runs many of the late Mr Scott's cinemas. This is one of those small town cinemas which my family and I visited in the late 1960s and which we remember with great affection. The Cinedrome appears from 1923 to 1939 in the KD; by 1969, in the KYB, it is known simply as The Cinema. The 1975 / 76 edition of the British Film & TV Year Book gives the name as the Royalty, by which time it had, as stated above, become one of the cinemas in the Charles Scott chain. The Cinema was also known at around this period as the Maxime. At that time it had 427 seats with 2-3 shows daily. I have in my possession a photograph (via Peter Hoare) taken at about this time showing Mr Scott on the steps of the cinema. [7.5.98]S

Dartmouth Cinema, not the original, but the last cinema to stand in Mayor's Avenue: interior of the Royalty.

The site of the various cinemas on Mayor's Avenue, Dartmouth, certainly the Royalty when I went there.

Exmouth Cinemas: 1920 - 1923

Forum / New Picture House   The Parade c1920 - ??   BE

This cinema appears for the first time in KD in 1923 and shows Bertram N. Thomas as manager. It is the first of the Exmouth cinemas to be shown on The Parade. By 1935, Leslie Bernard Thomas has taken over as the proprietor. The name disappears by the 1939 edition, by which time the Forum Cinema is shown at that address and Mr Leslie B.Thomas is still shown as the owner. The cinema did not appear in the 1969 edition of the KYB. The façade still survives but the building is now a bingo hall. It is difficult to gain any impression of the size of the cinema without inspecting the interior, which I have as yet been unable to do. [7.7.98]

Kings Theatre / Grand / Royal   Exeter Road c1917 - c1978   D

This was yet another cinema that changed names more than once during its lifetime. It appears in the 1917 KYB as The King's Theatre in Exeter Road. It does not appear in KD until 1923, by which time the Olden Brothers are shown as the proprietors. By 1935 it was owned by Glyn Hill, and by 1939 it had a change of owner and name: the owner was then C.H. Palmer and the new name was the Grand. In the 1969 KYB the name has changed again and the cin-

The Forum, Exmouth. Another of Devon's well hidden ex-cinemas, a well cared for example.

Site of the Grand Cinema, Exmouth. Nothing here to show that once cinema queues stood patiently in the rain waiting for their share of Hollywood dreams.

Holsworthy, The Market Hall Cinema. I am told that, during the renovations, a cinema ticket was found in what had been the auditorium.

ema is shown as the Royal. By this time it was owned by Mr Charles Scott, who was also running the Savoy in Exmouth as part of his circuit. The seating capacity in the 1960s was 401, with prices ranging from 4/- to 5/-. In the 1976 edition of the FTVYB, I found the first mention of car parks, one of which was for the Royal Cinema. Once again we can see the cinema as reflecting the social conditions of its time rather than its product, shown by the building itself plus the use of land for a car park. Following its closure, the cinema was demolished, and shops and flats were built on the site. At the time of writing I have found no picture of this cinema. It should be mentioned here that, in the 1917 KYB, three other venues are noted as well as the Kings Theatre. One of these is the Electric Palace, which I assume is the later Savoy. The other two are given as Public Hall and Pier Pavilion. I have found no other reference to these two venues and assume that they were short-lived and possibly part-time cinemas. [7.7.98]S

HolsworTHy CiNemas: 1920 - 1923

Market Hall Cinema   Market Hall, Exeter Road   c1920 - ??   BE

This was a cinema owned and run by the Holsworthy Urban District Council, and opened some time between 1919 and 1923. It appears in KD for the latter year but has disappeared by 1935. However, the mystery deepens as in the 1939 edition no cinema is shown but the entry reads as follows : 'Holsworthy Cinema Co Ltd (Stanley Rowland sec.) Holsworthy'.

Ilfracombe Cinemas: 1920 - 1923

The Scala   57 High Street 1920 - 1981   D

This cinema had a somewhat chequered career. It opened on Monday 20th December 1920 and closed on Saturday 28th February 1925. However, it re-opened on Monday 13th July 1925 under the same management as at the Palace. When the Palace closed in 1926, the Scala became Ilfracombe's premier cinema on the P.C.T. circuit (see above). In 1935 it became a Gaumont British Theatre. It retained the name Scala until December 1950 when it became known as the Gaumont. In 1964 the cinema was re-named the Clifton, being part of the Clifton circuit which also owned the Embassy in the town. A second screen, known as Clifton 2 (the main screen was known as Clifton 1)

Courtesy Tony Moss

Ilfracombe, The Scala: a view familiar to many patrons.

was opened in the old ballroom of the Scala in 1973: this was a 16mm projection system, not the normal 35mm system. Clifton 2 closed in 1980 and Clifton 1 on Saturday September 4th 1981. The building was demolished in 1983. Tragically, one man was killed during the demolition and another injured when a wall collapsed. The site is now occupied by flats and shops. It is ironic that the year after the building was demolished was also the time of a rise in cinema attendances, which trend has continued to the present. I would like to point out, at this stage, that I owe much of the detail here and in other sections on Ilfracombe to Mr Chris Vernon, who kindly supplied me with his own researches into the town's cinemas. [17.7.97]S

Author's collection

'What's on this week' at the Scala. We went anyway.

Moretonhampstead Cinemas:

The Rex   ?? address   ?? date   D

Until I found a photograph of the cinema, I had little information other than that it was known as 'The Little Green Hut' and was down the hill from the hospital. Mr Stafford Clarke tells me that the building was of galvanised iron construction, which is confirmed by the photograph. Mr Clarke, who was

Devon Books

Moretonhampstead The REX or 'Little Green Hut' as it was described to me by a former patron.

Author's collection

The Alexandra, formerly a Cornmarket, in Newton Abbot.

The Regent, Lyme Regis, another cinema in Peter Hoare's circuit. Although outside Devon, it is well worth a visit.

Author's collection

stationed at Harrowbeer during the war with R.A.F. 532 Squadron, says that the Rex was much frequented by American servicemen at that time. He also tells me that, although there was a camp cinema at Harrowbeer, it was very grotty, and the service personnel actually went to the cinema in Tavistock instead. I can find no reference to the cinema in KD up to 1939, neither does it appear in the KYB for 1969. Was this a cinema that came into being during the war years and failed to survive the departure of the service audience ?

Newton Abbot Cinemas 1920 - 1923

The Alexandra   Market Street   c1920s - present   CWC

When I spoke to the present owner of the Alexandra, Mr Peter Hoare, in October 1996, he was unable to give me an actual opening date for this cinema. However, it began life in the 1870s as the Corn Exchange. It was showing films during the silent period and was also used for the presentation of stage plays.

Mr Hoare says: *"It was built as a Corn Exchange, then after a time it was somewhat altered. It had quite reasonable stage facilities put in. I know it was used a lot for stage plays. Whether its use as a theatre pre-dates its use as a silent cinema I'm not certain. I'm a bit foggy about its early history. I know that the balcony was not put in until the twenties - pre-sound. A front was put on the balcony to make it look like an old Edwardian theatre, but that was actually false.*

[Mr Charles Scott, who ran several Devon cinemas in the post war period] became a manager of the Alexandra after his time in the RAF, the cinema being run at that time by the Newton Abbot Picture Company, who also ran the Imperial in Queen Street. They also had interests in cinemas in Paignton and Torquay. When the company was wound up, about 1960, Mr Scott put in a tender for the Alexandra and got it. Prior to this he was running the cinema in Cullompton. He then, with a mortgage, bought the cinema at Crediton. Later he acquired the leases of the two cinemas in Exmouth. [Together with Mr Peter Hoare he took out] a joint agreement with the Prince family to run the Riviera at Teignmouth. By the mid 1970s Crediton had gone and the proceeds partly bought the Regent at Lyme Regis. Mr Scott also acquired the lease of the cinema in Dartmouth. Mr Scott died about 12 years ago." [T.2.10.96]

Here we have a classic example of the local entrepreneur providing cinema for a large section of Devon cinema-goers, outside the two main urban areas of

Exeter and Plymouth. Mr Hoare has taken over some of Mr Scott's former empire, and runs four cinemas in Devon and two outside the county.

The cinema at an earlier date had seating for 560, which was then reduced to 370. It now has two screens with seating in the stalls: Screen 1, for 206 and in the balcony, Screen 2, for 127.   [2.10.96]

An early interior of the Alexandra, Newton Abbot.

The Empire Picture House   Lemon Road   c1920s - c 1930s   D

This seems to have been a short-lived venture, as the cinema was demolished and the site is now occupied by a car park. This site was pointed out to me early in 1998, when I was speaking on Devon Cinema History to the Newton Abbot Branch of the Devonshire Association. Ironically, the car park could be seen from the window of the building in which I was speaking. No more information to hand at this time.

Paignton Cinemas: 1920 - 1923

Electric Palace   Totnes Road   c1920s - c1960s   BE

This cinema opened as the Triangle Cinedrome, as noted earlier, but by 1923 was known as the Electric Palace by which name it continued to be known until it was closed in the 1960s. Mr J.J. Mann (Torbay Picture House) tells me that the cinema closed because queues caused problems with the then narrow street system. It was then owned by the same company that ran the Torbay Picture House. The building is still in existence but no longer has queues forming. Mr. Mann made the point that, had the decision to close been delayed, the change in the road system along with the rise in cinema-going from the mid 1980s, could have seen this cinema as a very profitable venture in the 1990s. [21.2.98]

Plymouth Cinemas: 1920 - 1923

Palladium Cinema   27 Ebrington Street   1922 - 1941   Bz

One of at least three cinemas in this street over the years, there is now no cinema here at all. The Palladium disappeared, with much of Plymouth, in the blitz in 1941. The Palladium, previously a roller skating rink, opened on December 11th 1922 with Eric von Stroheim's *Foolish Wives*. At that time its prices were 6d, 9d and 1/3d, with prices for children at 3d and 6d. Reginald Eady was the manager at this stage with Percy Gibson in office from 1934 to 1941, when the blitz brought an end to the story of this cinema. Photographs taken at the time show the façade still standing but the immediate interior, at least, reduced to rubble.

Plymouth: The Palladium, Ebrington Street, showing the result of the blitz.

People's Popular Picture Palace   Harbour Avenue   1921 - 1929   [?]

I have been unable to find any details of this cinema. It began at a time when many new venues sprang into use and seems to have fallen by the wayside with the coming of sound. Many of the smaller houses, who were just making a living in the silent days, were unable to afford the expense of wiring for sound and the extra cost involved in hiring sound films. Although sound came in, commercially, in 1927 its full effects were not felt, at least in this country, until 1929 / 1930. Britain's first sound film, Hitchcock's *Blackmail,* had its trade showing in June 1929. *The Jazz Singer* (which began it all in New York on October 6th 1927) was the first sound feature to be shown in London and opened at the Piccadilly Theatre on September 27th 1928. Even so, the sound revolution was both brisk and complete and there was no going back and even Chaplin was forced to see this, though he continued to produce 'silents' for some years.

Savoy ex- St. James Picture Palace   108 Union Street
1921 - 1941   D / Bz

Films had been shown at the St James Picture Palace since 1914, when the building was adapted for the showing of films, with seating for approximately 900 patrons. This was demolished, and in 1921 the Savoy cinema was opened on the site. This was a very large cinema with seating for 3,500. The original owners later sold out to the Gaumont British Picture Corporation. Sadly the cinema was to be yet another victim of the Plymouth blitz in 1941. The Gaumont firm in Britain, run by A.C. & R.C Bromhead, began in 1898 to distribute the films of Leon Gaumont. The firm was involved in both production and exhibition. In 1922, the Bromheads bought out the French interests and the firm became wholly British.

A graphic illustration of Plymouth during the blitz. No wonder the population needed to escape into the fantasy world of the movies.

Devon Books

The Criterion Kinema, closed and soon to become Weaver to Wearer. It was later destroyed in the blitz.

Courtesy Tony Moss

Criterion Kinema   13/14 Cornwall Street 1921 - 1939   Bz

The Criterion Kinema opened in 1921 and closed in 1939 when the site was acquired by 'Weaver to Wearer'. Sadly, the whole block was destroyed during the blitz, on the night of 20/21 March 1941. Contemporary photographs of the cinema show a very imposing façade with three arches abutting the pavement. Set back a few feet was the main entrance with details, doors etc. in the Art-Deco style. It appears to be at least a two storey building, but the photograph shows nothing above ground floor level. The proprietor was Mr Frank Pearce who continued as the owner until the Criterion Kinema was sold in 1939. The prices at this time, 1921, are given as 6d to 1/-. A later photograph taken after the raid of 20/21 March 1941 shows the building suffering from both blast and fire damage. The building next door is nothing but rubble.

Gaiety Cinema   193 Union Street 1922 - 1935   Bz

The Gaiety was another cinema to suffer from the name-change syndrome. Opened in 1922 as the Gaiety, it became the Carlton in 1936 and for the brief period, 1940 - 1941, it was known as the Embassy. It was under this name that it was destroyed in the blitz of 1941, along with much of Union Street. Even a cursory glance at the bomb plots of the Plymouth air raids will show just how much this area of Plymouth suffered during the war. The Gaiety, which opened with Mr M.P. Lowe as proprietor, was a medium-sized cinema with seating for about 400 patrons. It seems to have run continuous performances with prices ranging from 9d to 2/3d. So far I have been unable to trace any pictures of this cinema.

Teignmouth Cinemas: 1920 - 1923

The Riviera   1923 - 2000 The Den   Closed Feb 2000

As described above, it was in 1923 that the late Mr W. Prince acquired the building that is now known as the Riviera. He did much work on the building both at this time and later in the 1930s. Then Mr Prince's son, Mr Peter Prince, ran the cinema for many years, and he and his wife still live in the flat at the top of the building. At present, his two grandsons own the cinema, though it was one of four cinemas in the county run by Mr. Peter Hoare. The 1969 KYB gives the seating capacity as 901, but after the conversion in the early 1970s this figure had dropped by 1975-76 to 520. [2.10.96]

Riviera, Teignmouth: auditorium, showing sound grills.

Author's collection

Topsham Cinemas: 1920 - 1923

The Cosy   Fore Street 1921 - 1928   BE

The story of cinema in Topsham is the story of the Gould family, and I was fortunate to have a couple of long talks with the late Mr Lionel Gould in May 1996. Mr Lionel Gould told me of his family and the part that his father, Major Henry Charles Gould, played in providing cinema in the area. He described his father as 'a renaissance man'. He was by turn builder (his firm, H. Gould built Matthews Hall), fire officer, pioneer cinema proprietor, Freemason and a talented musician. The latter skill came into play when, for some special film, he would accompany the cinema pianist on his violin.

The first cinema that Major Gould opened was the Cosy Cinema off Fore Street in 1921 in what had been the old Victory Hall. This building appears to have begun life as a chapel. When I first visited the old Cosy (June 1998) it was then a glove factory, which has since closed. The Cosy ran on Wednesdays and

The Cosy Cinema, Topsham, one of Major Gould's circuit of rural cinemas in the 1920s and 1930s.

Saturdays, with performances at 6pm and 8.15pm, with prices of 5d., 9d., 1/- and 1/3d. Mr Lionel Gould had very fond memories of the two pianists who accompanied the silent films. The first was Miss Gladys Green, the station master's daughter and the second was a Mrs Drew who 'came all the way from Exeter'. Mr Lionel Gould himself acted, on occasions, as projectionist for his father. The main projectionist at Topsham was a Mr Fred Hoyle, who had worked at the Kings Hall, City Palace and Franklin in Exeter. That Mr Lionel Gould was part of a family team comes as no surprise and fits the national pattern. This was, perhaps, merely a carry over from the days when cinema was provided by travelling showmen, whose families often made up the entire workforce. The Cosy ran until 1928. We shall meet the Gould family again with the opening of Matthews Hall in Topsham when it became the new venue for cinema in the town. [5.6.96]

Torquay Cinemas:

Burlington   Union Street   1919 - 1953   [?]

For much information, illustrations, and publicity material on this cinema, I am indebted to Mr John Fleming, whose father, Mr Dudley Fleming, was the manager of the Burlington in the mid 1930s. Mr Dudley Fleming also ran cinemas in Cardiff and Bolton; when living in Africa he ran cinemas in Johannesburg, Queenstown and Krugersdorn. The publicity material from the Burlington of the mid to late 1930s shows just how hard managers in those days worked to bring in the patrons. This included full page spreads in the local paper, links with local shops, crossword puzzles with prizes of free cinema tickets, the importing of a monkey to advertise the latest 'Tarzan' film, and turning the foyer into an Advanced Dressing Station as publicity for the First World War drama *Forgotten Men*.

When the cinema opened, it was locally owned by the Burlington Picture House (Torquay) Ltd with William F. Gilley as the managing director. In 1935 the owners were the Regent Circuit Ltd, by which time Mr Dudley Fleming was the manager. By 1939 the cinema was in the hands of Associated British

Courtesy John Fleming

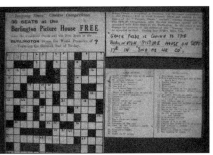

The Burlington, Torquay. Two examples of Dudley Fleming's brilliant use of advertising to pull in the patrons.

Courtesy John Fleming

Courtesy John Fleming

Burlington, Torquay. I wonder what happened to that dress and to the lady who won it?

Cinemas Ltd, and Mr Fleming had moved on. These changes mirror a national pattern with more and more cinemas being in the hands of fewer and fewer owners as the giant circuits moved in to take over the exhibition side of the industry. The cinema closed in 1953.

DEVON CINEMAS
1935

* Cinema

Ilfracombe * *
Lynton *
Braunton *
* Appledore
Barnstaple * *
Bideford *
South Molton *
Gt. Torrington *
Holsworthy
Tiverton * *
Okehampton *
Cullompton *
Crediton *
Honiton *
Chagford
EXETER * * * * *
Ottery St. Mary *
Tavistock *
Topsham *
Bovey
Axminster *
Princetown *
Sidmouth * *
Ashburton
Seaton *
Buckfastleigh *
Budleigh *
Newton Abbot * *
Exmouth * * * * * *
Dawlish
Devonport * * *
Teignmouth * * *
Plympton
Plymouth Ivybridge *
* * * * * * * Totnes *
Torquay * * * * * * * *
* * * * * * * Paignton * * * *
Brixham *
Kingsbridge * *
Dartmouth *
* Salcombe

N.B. These figures are taken from KYB 1935

Gordon Chapman: January 1999

By 1935 there are 34 towns with their own cinemas, and a total of 69 cinemas - figures taken from the Kine Year Book 1935. The pattern is that of the full range of cinema exhibition. The big circuits had now begun to make their mark: there were Gaumont cinemas in Barnstaple, Exeter and Plymouth, but Odeon cinemas had yet to appear on the scene. Alongside these new picture palaces, the older middle- and small-scale cinemas were still in operation, with local entrepreneurs continuing to play their part. The Noyce family of Kingsbridge and George Drake of Braunton are examples in this latter group. Note that the cinemas of this period are still concentrated in the south of the county, especially the holiday towns.

DEVON CINEMAS
1924 - 1935

In this period we move into the era of the Movie Palace and the giant Cinema Chains. It was this period that, during the 1930s, saw the emergence of the Odeon, ABC and Gaumont Circuits. Oscar Deutsch, the son of Jewish immigrants, was born in Birmingham in 1893. He acquired cinemas in Coventry by 1925, and soon had several others in the midlands. He built his first cinema, The Picture House, at Brierley in Staffordshire in 1928. Then, in 1930, he built and opened the first Odeon at Perry Barr in Birmingham. The name Odeon has had at least two explanations, first from the Odeon of Pericles suggested by one of Deutsch's partners, but more usually thought of as O.D.E.O.N, Oscar Deutsch Entertains Our Nation. Oscar Deutsch built up a cinema empire which, by the time of his death in 1941, covered the whole country. Deutsch was the first in this country to produce a 'House Style'. In his book *Cathedrals of the Movies*, David Atwell has this to say on the Deutsch empire:

> *"Deutsch wanted a cinema in every High Street of every town in the British Isles with a population of 25,000 or over, he wanted them designed quickly and built cheaply, and he wanted them to be as near identical as site limitations and the relevant local authorities would allow".*

Both George Cole and Andrew Mather designed cinemas for Deutsch. However, the Harry Weedon practice became his principal cinema architects. It was Robert Bullivant of that practice who designed the Exeter Odeon, which opened in 1937. Although plans were made to build an Odeon in Plymouth, a drawing of which appeared in the opening programme of the Exeter Odeon, the war intervened and nothing came of the plan. A similar story could be told of the building up of the Gaumont Circuit and Maxwells ABC empire. As we shall see, the county of Devon was to hold examples of all three circuits. Exeter had purpose-built Odeon and Gaumont cinemas, and ABC took over the old Savoy Cinema. Plymouth had a purpose-built Gaumont but, as stated above, the name Odeon was forced to appear on already existing cinemas. The coming of the Picture Palace, while bringing luxury to the cinema patron, caused many of the smaller houses to close. Being a rural county, Devon was not so badly affected as some in this respect.

The second major change for the cinema-goer at this time was the full-scale introduction of sound. Sound movies had been around since the beginning but they had all suffered from two major problems. These were amplification and synchronisation. The first of these problems was solved in 1906 with the invention of the audion tube by Dr Lee De Forest. I have been told that Dr Lee De Forest used both the Plymouth Pavilion and an army drill hall in Millbay Park during his early work on sound films, before he moved to London. I have found no confirmation of this information but it certainly seems possible. The synchronisation problem, like so many inventions, had many fathers but it was Fox Movietone News who first put the answer - sound on film - to practical commercial use. The film remembered as the first talkie, The Warner

Oscar Deutsch, founder of the Odeon Circuit, who died tragically in 1941: from the Exeter Odeon opening programme 1937.

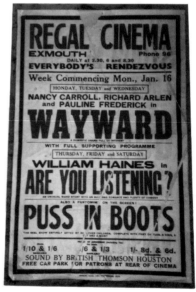

COMING OF SOUND: even the posters told the exciting news. Exmouth cinema poster.

Brothers' *The Jazz Singer,* starring Al Jolson (New York 6th October 1927) was in fact in the older, sound on disc system. Soon all films were produced on the sound on film system. Alfred Hitchcock's *Blackmail* of 1929 is credited as the first British 'talkie', though it began as a silent but was afterwards re-shot in sound. For a spoof account of the problems related to the coming of sound, there is no better instruction than the 1952 musical *Singing in the Rain.*

Battleship Potemkin, 1925, one of the world's greatest films. Very influential in technique.

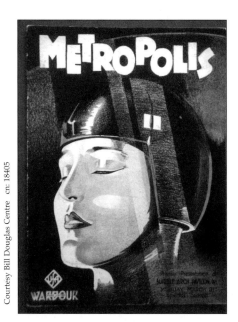

Metropolis. European films, directors and stars were moving to, and influencing Hollywood at this period.

All Quiet on the Western Front, which was, as Lew Ayres said, "The first film to show the enemy as people like us."

Some important films on release between 1923 and 1936:

Title		Director	Starring
Battleship Potemkin (1925)	(S) USSR	S.M. Eisenstein	
The Gold Rush (1925)	(S) US	Charles Chaplin	Chaplin, Georgia Hale
Metropolis (1925/6)	(S) G	Fritz Lang	Brigitte Helm, Alfred Abel
Ben Hur (2) 1926	(S) US	Fred Niblo	Ramon Novarro
The General (1927)	(S) US	Buster Keaton	Keaton, Marion Mack
The Crowd (1927/8)	(S) US	King Vidor	J. Murray, Eleanor Boardman
Sunrise (1927)	(S) US	F.W. Murnau	G. O'Brien, Janet Gaynor
All Quiet on the Western Front (1929)	(T) US	Lewis Milestone	Lew Ayres
Little Caesar (1930)	(T) US	Mervyn Le Roy	Edward G. Robinson.
Kameradschaft (1931) (T) G		G.W. Pabst	German & French cast
Private Life of Henry VIII (1932)	(T) UK	Alexander Korda	Charles Laughton
Triumph of the Will 1936	(doc) G	Leni Riefenstahl	

[(S) Silent film   (T) Talkie]

Axminster Cinemas : 1924 - 1935

Guildhall / Plaza   Anchor Hill c1925 - 1960s   BE

There seems to be some confusion regarding the naming of this cinema. A newspaper article states that the Plaza opened in the late 1920s and was later known as the Guildhall. However, two extant programmes would seem to suggest otherwise. A programme for December 1944 - January 1945 names the cinema as The Guildhall, while a programme for August 1958 gives it as the Plaza Cinema. No cinema is shown for Axminster in the 1969 KYB. (An interesting sidelight on cinema-going at that period is found on the front cover of the 1944/45 programme of The Guildhall: *'Messages: Doctors and other professional people expecting messages should leave their names at the Pay Box and with the attendants before taking their seats.'*)

At this time the Guildhall ran one performance starting at 7.30pm on Monday, Tuesday and Friday. Wednesday and Thursday had matinées at 2.30pm, and on Saturday there were three performances at 2pm, 5pm and 8 pm. The programme changed mid-week. By August 1958, performances were continuous from 2pm on Monday and Saturday, and from 4.45pm Tuesday to Friday. There were also Sunday showings with single performances at 7pm. Sunday cinema had long been a bone of contention in this country and in some areas remained so, despite new laws on the subject, with many local bodies fighting a strong rearguard action against what they saw as a profaning of the Sabbath. [5.6.98]

Charles Laughton's Henry VIII put British films firmly in the front rank of popular appeal.

Axminster, The Guildhall / Plaza: another cinema having a second lease of life as a public building.

*Axminster, Guildhall/Plaza.
Programmes for 1959.*

Barnstaple Cinemas: 1924 - 1935

Gaumont Palace / Astor   Boutport Street   1931 - present   CWC

On July 30th 1931 the local newspaper, the *North Devon Journal*, gave full coverage to the opening of this cinema and I can do no better than quote from that article:

Barnstaple's latest luxury cinema, the Gaumont Palace, will be formally opened to the public on Monday next by His Worship the Mayor of Barnstaple, Mr J.T. Dunn, J.P. The new Gaumont Palace in Boutport Street, stands on the site of the old Theatre

Axminster, Guildhall/Plaza. By 1961 it would seem that cost cutting was the order of the day; falling attendances were probably the cause here.

The Gaumont / Astor, Barnstaple. A difficult cinema to photograph because of its setting, but still looking much as it did when it opened on the 3rd of August 1931.

Gaumont / Astor, Barnstaple: a real 1930s façade.

Gaumont / Astor, close-up of the masks' decoration.

Royal....[which] has now given way to an up-to-date steel-framed fire-resisting Cinematograph Theatre, designed and equipped in accordance with the latest practice in lighting, heating and ventilation, picture projection and acoustics; the whole being carried out from designs and under the superintendence of Mr.W.H Watkins, F.R.I.B.A., Architect of 1 Clare Street, Bristol.

The new theatre is of the balcony type, and has seating accommodation for 1,124 persons, 702 on the ground floor and 422 in the balcony. The main entrance is in Boutport Street, but there is another entrance a few yards up Boutport Street, leading to what was formerly the yard of the Kingsley Hotel. The Kingsley Hotel having shared the fate of the old Theatre, its yard is now chiefly devoted to the separate entrance and waiting hall of the patrons of the front rows of the stalls.

The main elevation to Boutport Street is 70 feet wide, and is carried out principally in multi-coloured brick. On each side of the four pairs of entrance doors stand coupled pilasters of moulded brick, which carry the wide-spreading eaves of the central part of the elevation. Between them, and above the canopy projecting the entrance doors, are three windows of the balcony foyer; these are surrounded by an architrave in reconstituted Portland stone, and divided by fluted stone pilasters, whose capitals are grotesque masks. The whole is crowned by a steeply pitching roof of green glazed 'Cloister' tiles.

The Gaumont Palace's Grand Opening was on Monday 3rd August at 2.30pm when the main attraction was Eddie Cantor in *Whoopee*. The film is described as an *'All-Coloured Comedy Spectacle - Brilliant Musical Production with the Ziegfeld Beauties'*. Although the cinema, now known as the Astor, no longer functions under the Gaumont banner and has bingo as part of its programme, the exterior fortunately remains unchanged. So far I have been unable to view the interior, which is also described in detail in the article, but there must have been changes in order to run the bingo. An article in the *Western Morning News* [7.7.98], which speaks of a further possible change of use for the lower part of the building, tells us that the cinema runs in the upper floor of the building, and the bingo hall uses the bottom floor. I do have, thanks to Mrs Joyce Taylor, who worked at the Gaumont in the 1940s, a formal photograph of the staff and an informal 'snap' of the projection room crew taken on the roof of the cinema in September 1943. [17.7.97]

Courtesy Denis Knight

Mr Denis Knight (far left) using the canopy of the cinema to show his film on the wall opposite, the only film then in existence of the Lynton flood disaster. He collected over £100 that night for the Disaster Fund.

Courtesy Mrs Joyce Taylor

Gaumont, Barnstaple: the Staff of the Gaumont in 1943. Note the smart uniform, despite the war time shortages.

Courtesy Mrs Joyce Taylor

Informal shot of the projection staff, taken on the roof. 1943

Bideford Cinemas: 1924 - 1935

Palace Theatre   **Bridgeland Street c1930 - 1962**   **D**

The Palace Theatre appears for the first time in the 1935 edition of KD. This venue had previously been a Music Hall, which had shown films as part of its programme but, when music hall entertainment no longer attracted the crowds, it was converted into a cinema in the late 1920s or early 1930s. An old photograph of this building shows a most imposing structure with a Victorian Gothic look to it, even if having the name Palace painted across the façade was incongruous in the extreme. The building no longer exists. [16.7.97] S

Author's collection

The site of the former Palace - Bideford

The Plaza   Exeter Road 1935 - 1963   FE

When I visited Braunton in July 1997, I was delighted to note that the façade of the Plaza was basically unchanged; the owner, Mrs Dennis, kindly gave me a conducted tour of the building. This was then in three parts but the centre section of what had been the auditorium has been demolished. The façade, which is quite small and reminds one of the Savoy at South Molton, gives no clue to the size of the building it fronts. The main structure, which is larger than the façade would suggest, appears to be a metal frame with brick infill and rendered with an asbestos roof, common for this size of cinema at that time. The screen end remains, with its stage still in place as well as a number of the old cinema seats. The projection room is still there with the projection ports but all the equipment has gone. When it provided Braunton with its diet of Hollywood films, it was run by a Mr George Drake. [17.7.97]

I can best describe the interior by quoting directly from the information supplied by Mrs Anne Elliot in a letter dated August 11th 1998:

> Mr & Mrs Drake sat in the Box Office in the Foyer. Mrs Drake was very glamorous and looked like a film star! Red plush seats tip-up at the rear 2/-. Red plush seats tip-up in the middle 1/-. Entrance to these by the front entrance. Hard wood seats tip-up covered partly in red velvet and studded around the edges, 6d. [A heap of these cheap seats, still in their cast iron frames, was in the building when I visited in 1997.] Entrance to these by the fire exit at the bottom of the cinema. The fire door on the right hand side of the stage was the entrance and there were two red plush seats by this door for the manager and spouse or helper to sit. The cinema was very posh and kept very well. The walls were pale orange with a frieze. Stage curtains were deep red velvet with heavy fringes and a deep pelmet. There was a Fire Curtain which came down once every performance - a heavy roller blind type. At one stage Minnie Daniels was the usherette complete with atomiser which sprayed the air including the patrons with a highly perfumed freshener! This was in a very large and heavy container - coloured glass I believe. Chris Irwin was the ice-cream vendor. Frank Farrar, manager and pianist until the talkies came.

January 8th 1945 saw the last performance at the Plaza under George Drake's ownership. As stated in the section describing the early days of cinema in

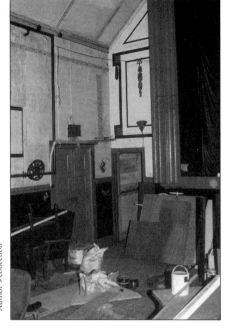

The Plaza, Braunton: screen end, prior to demolition.

The Plaza, Braunton, A very typical medium-sized cinema façade. The cinemas in South Molton and Holsworthy were both built at a similar date.

Braunton, Mr Drake took over the Plaza in January 1931. The cinema was then taken over by Mr Long, who ran the Plaza until it closed in 1964. When I drove past the ex-Plaza in August 1998, the rear sections appeared to have been totally demolished and houses built on the site. Fortunately the façade fronting the Plaza Confectionery shop remains.

Mr Long, the last purveyor of movie magic in Braunton, advertises Genevieve, a surprise hit.

Brixham Cinemas: 1924 - 1935

Electric Theatre   **Fore Street   c1931 - 1966**   **[BE]**

This cinema, first appearing in KD in 1935, stood in Fore Street. However, the 1923 edition gives an Electric Cinema (no street name) with a Miss J Dunsford as manageress. (See previous entry for the Regent) In 1935 and again in 1939 Mr. E.O. Ellis is given as the managing director of the Electric Theatre. The cinema was designed by W. Moxhay of St. Marychurch and built by Cooksley. The owner at this period was Mr Arthur Ellis. The Ellis family have been mentioned previously in connection with their cinema holdings. We are told in one publication that the first   film shown at the Electric Theatre was Hitchcock's 1935 classic, *Thirty Nine Steps* starring Robert Donat and Madeleine Carroll. When the cinema closed in 1966, after a showing of *The Rare Breed* (Maureen O'Hara and James Stewart), the cinema had been managed for some thirty years by Mrs W.A. Hexter. There was, I have been told, a cinema pianist named Mrs Hexter in the silent period. After the closure, the cinema was converted into a Somerfield supermarket.

Town Hall Cinema, Budleigh Salterton, a very attractive venue where, in 1997, the author saw Edwin Porter's 1903 classic The Great Train Robbery.

Town Hall/ Carlton/ Mayfair   Station Road   1929 - c1958:   BE

This cinema was one of many that ran as part of a multi-use situation. From information given by the late Mr Lionel Gould (interviewed 2.5.96), it seems that this was one of several venues used by his father Major Henry Gould for the showing of films, both silent and talkies. The cinema appears to have had three names, as suggested above, during its lifetime. The building, which is a very attractive one, is fortunately still extant.

Before moving to the Town Hall, [Major Gould]...*had been showing films in the old Drill Hall, known simply as The Cinema. This venture ran from 1925 to 1929. There was no electricity here so power for the projector and a couple of lights was provided by a generator run off the flywheel of a Buick motorcar. To stop the constantly running engine from boiling over, a rubber hose was run from a tap in the toilets of the Drill Hall to the radiator. Sadly, small boys had great fun pulling out the hose. This vehicle had been converted to a mini charabanc, seating about 8 people, and was used to take the staff and equipment to the various cinemas owned and run by Major Gould.'* [T 5.6.96] Interview with the son of Major Gould.

The rear view of another of Major Gould's small circuit.

Author's collection

In 1929 the Town Hall was built by Messrs Palmers. The foundation stone was laid by Lady Clinton on 25th June 1925. Major Gould ran this as a 'part-time' cinema from 1929 to 1931, in which year the local council took over the running of the cinema. In Major Gould's time the Budleigh Town Hall ran as a cinema on Friday evenings, with the same films as shown in Topsham on Wednesdays and Saturdays. This venue ran for many years, indeed until after the Second World War, being known at different times as the Carlton and the Mayfair. In 1997 a board showing admission prices for the Mayfair was discovered in the loft space. Prices shown on the board are 10d, 1/6d, 1/9d and 2/3d. [15.10.96+]

CREdITON CINEMAS:

The Palace   East Street   c1930 - c1960s   BE

This building still stands and from the outside looks much as it did when it opened in the heyday of cinema-going. Prior to the opening of the Palace, films had been shown in Crediton for a number of years in the Town Hall. The Palace however was a purpose-built cinema which, according to the plans kindly supplied by the present owner Mr John Gregory, seated exactly 365 patrons. As the present owner of the premises (now a snooker hall) Mr John Gregory said, *"You could have a different seat for every day of the year."* [T 4.12.96]

Courtesy John Gregory

The Palace, Crediton: a painting of the cinema, which is unique in my experience. There must be others out there somewhere.

Courtesy Albert Labbett

The Palace, Crediton, when still a working cinema.

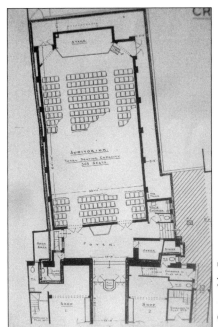

Courtesy John Gregory

The Palace, Crediton: seating plan. You could have a different seat every night of the year as there were 365.

The building was a single storey edifice facing directly onto East Street. Mr Gregory has altered the interior to its present use but has otherwise left the building alone. The projection box is still there with the port covers still in working order along with the switch gear. There is no equipment left in the building but one can still see an old poster on the auditorium wall, and a painting, by Len Boddy, of the building as it appeared in 1933. The film being shown at the Palace in this painting was *Up for the Cup* (1931) with Sidney Howard and Joan Wyndham. Until 1939 the Palace was owned by The Crediton Cinema Co. Ltd. At one stage, after the Second World War, the Palace was bought by Mr Charles Scott and became part of his local circuit which also included cinemas in Newton Abbot, Cullompton, Exmouth, Dartmouth and Teignmouth. The cinema was still operating under Mr Scott in 1969 (KYB), though now known as the Regal. At that date the seating was still given as 365, with prices of 3/6d and 4/6d. There were two shows daily with three on Saturdays. Also by this date cinemascope had been fitted. The cinema had closed by 1975 (FTVYB). [4.12.96]

At this point it is appropriate to include a letter that I received in June 1998 from Mrs D. Blackmore of Crediton. Before and during the war Mrs Blackmore worked for the Gaumont British Picture company.

Dear Mr Chapman

[It] concerns the beginning of the Second World War when the Gaumont British Pictures, then owned by the Ostrer brothers (Maurice and Mark), bought a mansion in Crediton, to where they evacuated the whole of this film empire's headquarters from London, staff included.

The daily takings were sent down overnight on the train, which incidentally was the newspaper train heading for Devon and Cornwall. So the whole of the country's cinema takings were received in Crediton the next day to be dealt with by the various accountants, auditors etc. One large room in the house was set aside for Burrows adding machines and very noisy they were. A cinema and dance hall was built in the grounds and chalets erected for their employees.

You may not have heard of the Ostrer brothers but you will remember I am sure James Mason, the actor who married Pamela Ostrer [a daughter] and who subsequently had a daughter called Portland....

Mrs Blackmore tells me that all traces of this enterprise have now disappeared and I am very grateful to her for bringing this little known information to my attention.

Author's collection

Author's collection

Although there is now nothing left of the Gaumont's presence in Crediton, we can still find their logo on these seats in the Carlton Cinema in Okehampton. Very Art-Deco.

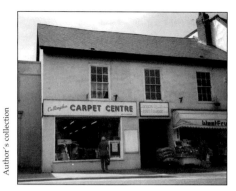

Cullompton, site of the former Regal cinema, which was, for a time at least, another of Charlie Scott's cinemas.

Cullompton Cinemas: 1920 - 1923

Regal   High Street c1930s - c1970s   BE

The Regal in Cullompton appears to have been opened in the 1930s and closed in the early 1970s. It appears in KD for 1935 & 1939 and in the KYB for 1969, but does not appear in the FTVYB for 1975-6. In the 1960s it was one of the cinemas owned by Mr Charles Scott, who acquired this cinema while he was managing the Alexandra at Newton Abbot. The seating at this time is given as 300. There were two shows daily, with three on Saturdays and a single Sunday performance; the seat prices were 4/6 and 3/6. In the 1930s the cinema was owned by the Cullompton Cinema Co. Ltd. The building, which has been converted into two shops, appears from the street to be a 19th century double-fronted house. Unfortunately I was unable to view the interior on this visit. [11.9.97] Since the above was written, I have been told of an earlier cinema in Cullompton, but so far I have been unable to visit it, if in fact it is still extant.

Dawlish. Site of the former cinema, which too often is all that is left, not one brick upon another.

Dawlish Cinemas: 1924 - 1935

The Scala   Albert Street c1930 - c1960   [D]

The **Scala** was the second of two cinemas in Dawlish, the earlier cinema being in Chapel Street and run by a Mr Walford. The Scala occupied the site now taken over by Barclays Bank and the Library. The proprietor in 1935 is given as A.R. Phern, who also owned the Carlton and Lyceum cinemas in Teignmouth at this time. The KYB 1940 credits the Scala with a proscenium measuring 26 feet, four dressing rooms, and with seating for 400. By 1951 the seating had been reduced to 370. Sadly, there is now no sign of either cinema at street level and so far I have been unable to locate any photographs of these two venues. [1996]S

Devonport Cinemas: 1924 - 1935

The Alhambra   Tavistock Street 1924 - 1932   Bz

This cinema, which showed films in the silent period, seems little known. Even Pat Ghillyer has little to say on this short-lived cinema. It was not on Fore Street with the Electric, Tivoli and Forum, but was to be found further down on Tavistock Street, which ran off Fore Street opposite Marlborough Street. Although it is given as closed in 1936, there is no obvious reason for closure at this date. It could be due to competition as it seems too late to owe its demise to the coming of sound in the late 1920s. The building was destroyed in the blitz of 1941.

The Hippodrome   Princes Street 1929 - 1941   Bz

The Hippodrome was actually opened in 1907 as a variety theatre. The theatre re-opened as a cinema in December 1929. It had seating for around 2000 with prices at this time from 6d to 2/6d. Just prior to the Second World War the Hippodrome became part of the County Cinema circuit, which in turn became part of the Odeon empire. It was so damaged in the blitz of 1941 that it never re-opened. Photographs show a very imposing 3-4 storey brick building with a rather sober façade and a canopy stretching the full width of the main façade. A single storey pit entrance, to the right of the main building, is not covered by this canopy. A possible case of class distinction ? The projection box was built on the roof and the new Hippodrome opened with the 1929 M.G.M. musical *Broadway Melody*, starring Charles King, Anita Page and

Hippodrome, Devonport. A magnificent façade that betrays its former role in the entertainment world.

Bessie Love. This was the very first 'talking' musical to come out of Hollywood, and probably anywhere in the world. After the war, the site was used by the Salvation Army for their Red Shield House.

Exeter Cinemas : 1924 - 1935

The Hippodrome (1908) / Plaza   London Inn Square
1931 - 1942   Bz

The Hippodrome theatre opened in 1908 and was part-owned by Fred Karno, who was born in Exeter. Charlie Chaplin was part of Karno's *Mumming Birds* troupe at this time and I have copies of photographs showing a board outside the Hippodrome advertising this show. I have recently been assured that Chaplin was in the troupe that played in Exeter at this time. In 1910 he sailed to America with Karno's *Mumming Birds* and found world fame as 'The Little Tramp.' The Hippodrome was re-named the Plaza and opened as a full-time cinema on the 16th February 1931. It opened with the film *King of Jazz (1930)* with John Boles and Bing Crosby, and featuring Paul Whiteman and his orchestra. Prices ranged from 6d to 2/4d. The manager at the time of the opening was Mr Lattimer, though by 1935 Mr A.E. Firebrace held the post. The usual photograph shown of the Plaza was at a time when the main attraction was *Casino de Paree*, starring the then husband and wife Al Jolson and Ruby Keeler. The same photograph clearly shows a sign for a café, which was part of the Plaza cinema. The cinema fits in well with the surrounding architecture, while still showing clear signs of the former Hippodrome façade. The

Courtesy DEI

The Plaza cinema, Exeter, a conversion of the earlier Hippodrome, in which Fred Karno had an interest.

Courtesy Dick Passmore

The Savoy (Exeter) under construction, with the Plaza cinema already in operation in the background.

large illuminated sign, *PLAZA*, on the façade is reported to have been the first neon sign in the city. Another photograph taken at the same time but from a slightly different angle, shows the Savoy cinema under construction. Despite being so close, the Savoy survived the blitz but the Plaza did not - it was lost in 1942 in the Baedeker raids on the city. [1996]S

Gaumont   11/ 12 North Street   1932 - 1967   BE

The first of the big chain cinemas to be built in Exeter, the Gaumont opened in 1931. Despite some damage in the blitz in 1942, this building is still standing. It was converted to bingo after it closed as a cinema in 1967. There was some

PLEASURE AT THE PLAZA

A delightful half day can always be spent by a visit to the Matinee Performance at 2 and a Tea Party in the Plaza Café afterwards.

The Plaza Café being so central is greatly appreciated by a large number who need refreshment at mid-day and have business in the vicinity.

Our Electric Gramophone adds gaiety to pleasant meals and we claim the quickest service in the City.

CAFÉ PLAZA

Hours:
10 a.m. to 10 p.m. Daily
12.30 to 9 p.m. Sundays

Courtesy Richard Davin

The Plaza (Exeter) Café. The cinema café was very much part of 'going to the movies', and not only in the bigger venues. Seaton Regal certainly boasted one.

The Gaumont (Exeter). As it is set back from the street, it is a difficult building to photograph.

The Staff of the Gaumont in full uniform, c.1950.

King's Hall (Exeter) seen from across the river.

damage done to the fabric of the building during the blitz but it was restored after the war. In 1998, it was still possible to walk in and see the interior much as it would have appeared to patrons in its heyday. Like the much smaller Tivoli in Tiverton, the Gaumont is set back from the road and one enters through a rather imposing gateway, which, like the cinema itself, is built of brick. The architect was Mr. W.H. Watkins F.R.I.B.A. of Bristol, who also designed the Gaumont in Barnstaple among many other cinemas. It was a 1500 seater cinema and very well appointed. The staff all wore a uniform, as was normal at that period. A copy of a staff photograph, given to me by Mrs H.M. Ogg of Bradninch, shows 12 ladies in uniform, 10 in street clothes, 4 men in uniform, 7 not in uniform. The manager sits centre front in dinner jacket and bow tie. One assumes that the non-uniformed staff worked behind the scenes in office and projection roles. The programme is given as continuous, 2pm - 10.30pm during the week and 3.15pm to 9.30pm on Sundays. The photograph, which includes Mrs Ogg's brother Mr Harry Parsons, was taken, she tells me, in the late 1940s or early 1950s.

The cinema opened with *Sunshine Susie,* starring Jack Hulbert and Owen Nares. This was a re-make of a German film, *Die Privatsekretarin*; re-makes were in vogue around this time. Many British film makers spent time working in the German studios, among them Alfred Hitchcock, and there was also a movement in the opposite direction. It was this cinema that was banned from showing the classic *Frankenstein,* and horror fans had to travel to Topsham to see it. This they did 'in droves', as Mr Lionel Gould recalled for me, when talking of the days when his father Major Gould, who ran the cinema, showed it. [18.3.96]

Kings Hall   13/14 Okehampton Street   1925 - 1936   BE

This building, which in part still stands in Okehampton Street, has quite a varied history, and that quite apart from its role as a cinema. It would appear that this building was opened as a multi-use parish hall in 1912. From a very early date this building was used for the showing of films, all silent in those days, of course. One should, perhaps, qualify the term 'silent'. As we have seen with the tiny Cosy Cinema at Topsham, there was always at least a piano to accompany the antics of Fatty Arbuckle or the tears of Lillian Gish. In larger halls there were trios and even larger ensembles. When *Birth of a Nation*, still known at that stage as *The Clansman*, opened in Clune's Auditorium in 1915, the film was accompanied by the entire Los Angeles Symphony Orchestra. The Kings Hall opened as a full-time cinema in 1925, and some authorities state that this was the first cinema in Exeter to show 'talking' films. By 1936 it could no longer compete with the newly-opened picture palaces, such as the Palladium and the Gaumont, and so it closed. It then became a variety theatre until it was taken over at the start of the Second World War by J. Wippell and Co. for the production of parachutes. After the war it became a store for Ferodo Ltd. Photographs of the interior taken at this time show a building with distinct Victorian overtones, especially in the ironwork of the first floor gallery. For some time now the building has been used as a night club. [17.11.96] A further change of use is reported in the Express & Echo [12.8.98] where it is stated that the building had become the Riverside Christian Centre.

EXMOUTH CINEMAS: 1924 - 1935

Regal   St. Andrews Street   c1930s - ??   BE

When I visited the site of this ex-cinema in July 1998, I was struck by the size of the building. It is of brick construction and gives an impression of permanence. It now appears to be part of a complex of buildings and it is not easy to

Exmouth, the Regal Cinema, now looking rather sad.

decide just what constituted the original structure and what has been added at a later date. The building, or rather part of the building, is now 'Samantha's Night-Club'. The Regal appears in the 1935 and 1939 editions of KD, but does not appear in the 1969 edition of the FTVYB. I have no further details of this cinema at present. [7.7.98]

Holsworthy Cinemas : 1923 - 1935

Holsworthy Cinema   Bodmin Street   c1933 - c1962   BE

When I visited Holsworthy in August 1998, I was delighted to see that, although the building was no longer a cinema, it was still serving the arts in the form of a local amateur theatre. I was unable to view the interior on this occasion. The façade, which has echoes of both the Savoy at Braunton and the Savoy at South Molton, is very much in the 'modernistic' style of the 1930s. Programmes for 1933 / 34 give prices ranging from 7d to 1/10, children 4d and 7d. By 1937 the prices had dropped and ranged from 6d to 1/6d. One is tempted to see this drop as the result of the depression and large scale unemployment at this period. Performances were: Monday, Wednesday, Thursday and Saturday, continuous from 6pm, Tuesday and Friday at 7.45pm. On Carnival Day there were three special performances (90 minutes) at 6pm,

Regal Cinema (Exmouth). Lew Ayres is best known for his role in All Quiet on the Western Front. Note the adverts for both car park and the new 'Talkies'.

Holsworthy Cinema, looking splendid after refurbishment for its new role as a theatre.

Holsworthy Cinema programme for May-June 1937.

Holsworthy Cinema detail from 1937 programme.

The Devonia Cinema, Honiton. The façade: all that is left after the fire in the 1950s.

8.15pm and 9.45pm, prices 9d and 1/3. The programme for November 16th, 17th and 18th is *The Midshipmaid* starring Jessie Matthews, in which John Mills made his first screen appearance. This is one of the only cinemas which at this time was advertising a FREE CAR PARK; I find this unusual at this early date but, with a scattered clientele from a largely rural area, it does make sense. Advertisements on the programmes make interesting reading. For example: 'The popular Ford - £100 (1937)' and in 1938 'Buy a Ford 10, develops over 30 B.H.P. Tax £7/10/0. Prices from £145 at Works' and 'A fine range of 1937 Suitings, prices 42/- to 85/-'. And in the May - June 1937 programme we read: 'Special Displays of Coronation Novelties in Men's Wear - The height of Fashion at reasonable prices.' [6.8.98]

Honiton Cinemas: 1924 - 1935

The Devonia   205 High Street   c1930 - c1959   FE

The Devonia at the bottom of High Street replaced the previously mentioned Cinema at the top of the town. The Cinema was, as was common in the early period of cinema exhibition, a conversion. The Devonia was a purpose-built brick cinema in the rather austere style of the period. The façade and what would have been the front offices remain, together with the interior iron staircase to the projection box. The present owner also possesses the stainless steel

The Devonia in its heyday as the best cinema in town. This was yet another cinema that closed following a fire.

letters that once graced the façade. The cinema was gutted by fire in the 1950s, and never re-opened as a cinema. A street photograph of the lower end of High Street in Honiton, taken in 1959, which shows the Devonia, appears on page 30 of Les Berry & Gerald Gosling's *Around Honiton.* A view in the same book, c1920, shows the Cinema at the top of High Street. [16.4.96]

Kingsbridge Cinemas: 1924 - 1935

The Palace / Early Cinema	**Piggy-Wigg Lane/ Quay Lane**
No dates	**BE**

I have included The Palace cinema at this point as I have, at present, no dates or details and felt that it was best to include it here with the later Regal cinema. From J.J. Mann of Paignton I heard of an early cinema in Kingsbridge sited in Piggy-Wigg Lane, though when I visited the area in August 1998 I was told that this narrow alley is now called Quay Lane. Mr Tim Blyth of Kernborough, near Kingsbridge, confirmed that this early cinema, which he named The Palace, did exist. It was sited near the small Lloyds Bank just off the Quay. The building is a large stone built structure, which at one time was the headquarters of the local Boy Scouts. Double doors facing this narrow lane were the main entrance to the cinema, which was on the first floor. I have been unable, at this stage, to uncover any other relevant information. [1998]

The early cinema in Quay Lane, Kingsbridge.

The Regal Cinema	**The Island c1930s - 1974**	**BE**

This is a cinema that I remember with great affection. When holidaying at Bantham, near Kingsbridge, in the 1960s and 70s, this was the cinema to which my wife and I went with our three children. My children remember it particularly as 'the cinema with no toilets', for which facility one had to go outside and across the road - no fun on a blowy, rainy night with the wind howling up the estuary!

The Regal Cinema, Kingsbridge. Happy memories: my family and I were regular patrons here until it closed

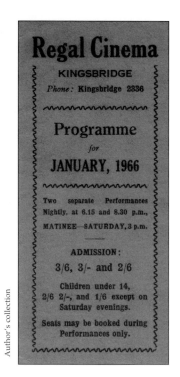

Regal Cinema

KINGSBRIDGE

Phone: **Kingsbridge 2336**

Programme

for

JANUARY, 1966

Two separate Performances
Nightly, at 6.15 and 8.30 p.m.,
MATINEE—SATURDAY, 3 p.m.

ADMISSION:

3/6, 3/- and 2/6

Children under 14,
2/6 2/-, and 1/6 except on
Saturday evenings.

Seats may be booked during
Performances only.

*The Regal Cinema, Kingsbridge:
programme January 1966.*

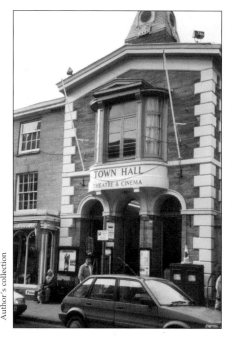

*The Town Hall and now the Reel Cinema
(opened 2000), which carries on a long
tradition of cinema going in Kingsbridge.*

The cinema was owned and run by the Noyce family, from its opening in the 1930s until its closure in 1974. The 1969 edition of the KYB gives the seating capacity as 284, with prices from 1/6d to 4/-. The address given in KD is The Island, as the cinema is situated in a triangle of roads. The building still stands, though changed superficially on the outside, with the interior now used for various purposes. Mr Tim Noyce tells me that the cinema was built on the site of his grandfather's house. [1966 +]

Town Hall Cinema & Theatre   Fore Street   1980s - PT PT/CWC

With the demise of the Regal in 1974, Kingsbridge, like so many market towns in Devon, was left without a cinema. This was partly remedied by converting part of the Town Hall into a small but well-developed and well-run theatre-cum-cinema, with cinema performances two nights per week. [1997] This venue re-opened as a full-time cinema, the Reel Cinema on 20th May 2000, with a showing of the film *Galaxy Quest* - offering free popcorn to the cinema audience. The new owner is local businessman Mr Phil Pritchard. The Reel Cinema is a 200 seater cinema with a café. At a time when the super multiplex cinemas hold centre stage, it is good to see a return to the days when the local entrepreneur provided our screen entertainment. Long may it prosper.

PAIGNTON CINEMAS: 1924 - 1935

Palladium/ Odeon   Torquay Road   1932 - (1939) -c1950s   D

The Palladium opened on Saturday 31st December 1932. The opening ceremony was performed by G.H.K. Kingdom Esq., J.P. and the main attraction was Jessie Matthews in *The Midshipmaid*. Lower down the cast list, as Midshipman Golightly, was John Mills in his first film role. The programme on that occasion also included *The Palladium News*, the Disney cartoon *Trees and Flowers - a Silly Symphony in Colour* and Laurel & Hardy in *County Hospital*. Melbourne Holman entertained on the Wonder Christie Organ. There were three performances daily at 2.30pm, 5.45pm. and 8.30pm. with prices for the stalls ranging from 7d to 1/6d and the balcony from 1/6d to 2/-; children half price at matinées only. The cinema also boasted a café on the first floor. The building was an impressive one on a corner site. It was, as stated in the opening programme, associated with '*the All-British cinema controlling organisation known as County Cinemas Ltd.*' The architect was Mr William Wolff of Paignton and the general contractor was also from Paignton, Mr R.M. Ely. It had a seating capacity of 1,100. Safety is again emphasised in the description given in the opening programme, which states: *Patrons are invited to note the arrangements made for safety in the event of emergency. Owing to erection upon a corner site the provision of exits is actually in excess of the exacting requirements of regulations and the 'Palladium', if packed to capacity, could be emptied comfortably in two minutes. The theatre is fireproof. With the exception of the doors, the building itself is of brick, steel and concrete ... It is practically British-made throughout. The interior was also designed by the architect. The power to the cinema was provided by 'The Paignton & District Electric Supply Company'. The Palladium Café is open to the Public from 2.30 pm. to 10 pm daily...All high - grade Chocolates and Cigarettes can be obtained from the Waitresses or Theatre Attendants....Patrons anticipating an urgent Telephone message or call can obtain from the Pay Box a Special Form which will ensure immediate attention should such a message or call come through.....Always at your service, CLEMENCE R. TREE, Director and General Manager.*

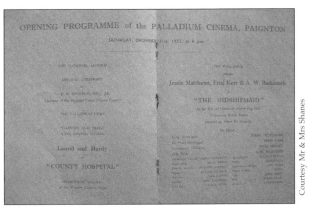

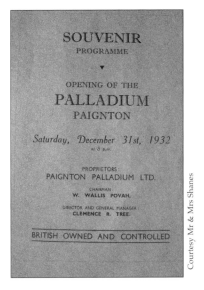

Most of the above information comes from the Opening Programme, owned by Mr J Shanes, who kindly allowed me to make a copy.

In 1939 the Palladium became part of the Oscar Deutsch empire and was re-named Odeon. It remained thus until it closed as a cinema in the 1950s when it became a bingo hall. The building was demolished in 1988 and a block of flats now stands on the site.

The Regent   Station Road 1932 - 1983   D

From photographs taken on the opening day, the Regent looks to have been an imposing building. It was built, like the Palladium, on a corner site, with a tower centre bearing the word REGENT and a canopy running the full length of the building. I was told by an ex assistant-projectionist of the Regent that it was quite a small cinema. However the KYB 1940 gives the seating as 745, a figure that remained fairly constant through the years. In 1976 that figure had fallen to 654, reflecting the drop in cinema attendances during this period. Prices in 1940 were ranging from 6d to 2/-, by 1969 these had risen to a range of 5/- to 6/6. The building was put up for sale in 1987 and later demolished and the site redeveloped. I have no further information on this cinema at the present time.

Top left: Palladium/Odeon, Paignton. Drawing from the opening programme. The building was demolished, now flats stand in its place.

Top centre and above: Palladium/Odeon, Paignton. Opening programme.

The Regent, Paignton, taken on opening day.

The Regent, Paignton, Illuminated for the opening.

Roseville / Argyll   56 Mutley Plain   1925 - 1926 - 1927   D

This is a cinema with a fairly short history. It began life as the Mutley Plain Cinedrome in 1914, when the proprietor was Mr W. Linsdell. In 1925 it was re-named the Roseville. However, this was a short-lived venture and the cinema changed its name again in 1926 when it became the Argyll, which in turn closed in 1927. I am not certain why this cinema closed, it is too early for the coming of sound to have been a factor, but it has been suggested that, as a small cinema, it was unable to compete with the larger Belgrave Cinema. A supermarket now stands on the site.

The proposed new Odeon for Plymouth, which was never built. Opening Programme, Exeter Odeon.

Courtesy Dick Passmore

Gaumont Palace/Gaumont   151 Union Street   1931 - 1962   BE

This typical 1930s picture palace replaced the earlier Andrews New Picture Palace, which had opened in 1914. This building was demolished in 1931 and replaced by the new Gaumont Palace in that year. Later the 'Palace' part of the named was dropped and it was known simply as the Gaumont. In 1962, the name Gaumont was dropped and it was known for a time as the Odeon. When Rank obtained control of both the Odeon and Gaumont circuits, and with audiences falling off, it became common practice, where both an Odeon and a Gaumont existed in close proximity, to close one of the cinemas. This was often the Gaumont. In this case, as there was no purpose-built Odeon in the city, the name Odeon was transferred from the cinema (ex- Regent) in Frankfort Street which had carried the Odeon name from 1940 to the Gaumont in Union Street.

Author's collection

The Gaumont Palace/ Gaumont, Union Street, Plymouth..

The Gaumont has a very imposing façade of brick, which just shouts 'cinema' to any passer-by. It was designed by the prolific cinema architect W.H. Watkins, of Bristol, who was also responsible for the Gaumonts in Exeter and Barnstaple. The Plymouth Gaumont had seating for 2,300, with 1,500 in the stalls and 800 in the circle. It was built by McLaughlin and Harvey. The cinema was equipped with a stage and dressing rooms. It also featured a Compton Organ. Photographs of the interior, though in black & white, give a very clear impression of the luxury awaiting patrons. Though a large cinema, the Gaumont did not have a café or, as some cinemas of the period, a dance hall. A writer in the Western Evening Herald (14th November 1931) had this to say of the new cinema : *'Tall, fluted columns which, under floodlighting, appear to stretch from Union Street Plymouth into deep darkness, invite passers-by into the new Gaumont Palace to discover what wonders are hid by the alluring and mysterious blackness.'* The cinema was officially opened on the 16th November 1931 by the Mayor of Plymouth, Alderman G.P. Dymond, who was supported by Viscountess Astor, M.P. The cinema opened with *The Ghost Train* starring Jack

Hulbert and Cicely Courtneidge. Also on the programme that day was *Almost a Divorce* with Sidney Howard and Nelson Keyes. [16.1.97]

Grand Theatre   Union Street   1889 - (1935) - 1941   Bz/ D

The Grand Theatre, some traces of which remain (1997) in Union Street, opened on Boxing Day 1889. At that time it was a 1300-seater theatre. It seems to have enjoyed a long and successful career as a theatre, but as theatre attendances diminished in the face of competition from the cinema, it was forced to follow public taste. In 1935 the Grand became a cinema and remained so until it was severely damaged in the blitz in 1941. It was later used as a warehouse. Judging from photographs I have seen, the building seems to have been very imposing and it was obviously a loss to the city when it was demolished after the war. [16.1.97]S

The Grand Theatre, later a cinema, demolished 1962.

Regent/ Odeon   Frankfort Street   1931 - (1940) - 1962   D

The Regent, a purpose-built cinema, stood in Frankfort Street and, with 3,254 seats, had the largest seating capacity of any cinema in the city. The cinema opened on Saturday 21st November 1931, with Chaplin's film *City Lights*, starring Chaplin and Virginia Cherrill; the film got rather mixed notices from the critics. This cinema also had stage facilities and dressing rooms. It was an independent cinema, owned by Regent Cinemas (Plymouth) Ltd., at least one of whose directors, William Mumford, was also involved in the public transport business - Mumfords Motors. Prices at this stage ranged from 7d to 2/- . No organ seems ever to have been installed in this cinema, which is strange considering its size. Later, the Regent passed into the County Cinemas circuit and later, on the 17th June 1940, became a part of the Odeon empire. As has been stated earlier, there were plans afoot for a purpose-built Odeon in Plymouth, to have been sited in Union Street. Whether it was the acquisition of the Regent or the coming of war that caused these plans to be changed, I am unable to say. Pre-war photographs show the Regent, tall and bright, standing out from the surrounding buildings. The word REGENT forms part of the décor of the façade above the three large windows, and appears again above the building, in what looks to have been neon lettering on a frame. The Regent was known from 1940 onwards as the Odeon, which survived the blitz but not the march of progress, and finally closed on the 8th September 1962. The Second World War brought a measure of fame to the cinema: Glenn Miller gave concerts for American servicemen in this cinema and in May 1944 General Montgomery used the building to talk to the troops stationed in the area. [1995]S

Plymouth, Regent / Odeon, Frankfort Street.

Plaza   Treville Street (36, Bretonside) 1934 - (1964) - 1981   BE

The Plaza, though no longer a cinema, still stands in what is now known as Bretonside, close to the bus station. The exterior looks much as it did when it opened in February 1934. This was a cinema of medium size with seating for 933 patrons. The architect was J. Hammick. Prices here were on a par with other cinemas in the city, ranging from 6d to 1/6d. Soon after its opening, the cinema became a part of the ABC (Associated British Cinemas) circuit, owned by the Scottish entrepreneur John Maxwell, who had entered into cinema exhibition in 1912, and whose ABC circuit owned 118 cinemas by 1930. The cinema continued in operation throughout the war years and remained in the ABC circuit until 1964, when it was sold and re-named Studio 7. When the cinema was acquired by Shipman & King in 1976, it reverted to its original name of Plaza. It closed in October 1981. When I

The Plaza when still a working cinema, showing a film that does not appear in any popular reference book.

Author's collection

The former Plaza cinema, typical of its period, but one wonders how long it can survive.

visited the building in 1997, it was being used as an Indian restaurant and a snooker hall. With much redevelopment in the area, one wonders just how long this building will remain. [16.4.97]

Salcombe Cinemas: 1924 - 1935

The Lyric   **Market Street c1935 - c1950s**   **D**

So far I have been unable to discover any real information about this cinema other than its name and the fact that it was demolished during a road widening scheme. The KYB shows that it was open by 1935. Prices at that time ranged from 4d to 1/10d, with seating for approximately 200. A photograph on display in the Salcombe Museum shows the rear of the building. From this photograph it would appear to have been a small cinema, similar in seating to many similar small venues in the county.   [1997]S

The Lyric Cinema, Salcombe, of which I can only find this rear view, taken during a celebration. The building was demolished in 1963.

Courtesy Salcombe Museum

Seaton Cinemas: 1924 - 1935

The Regal   **Fore Street c1935 - 1972**   **D**

The Regal in Seaton was open by 1935 (KYB 1935: KD 1935) and continued to operate as a cinema until its closure in 1972. The building then stood empty until it was demolished in 1975. As was to happen many times in this period, local pressure was brought to bear to save the cinema, but to no avail. When looking back on this closure and many others, it is all too easy to allow sentiment to cloud the real issue. No cinema can continue in business unless it makes money: although cinema simply means entertainment to the patron, to the owner, especially if it is a small concern, it means his livelihood. Therefore, unless the public use the facility and provide that livelihood, it must and will close down.

The Regal appears from photographs to have been a pleasant building, typical of many small town cinemas of the period. When it opened, the cinema had an upstairs tea lounge, though I am not sure how long this civilising aspect lasted. Prices in 1935 ranged from 6d to 1/8d, with seating for 588 patrons. At that stage the cinema was owned by the Seaton Cinema Co. Ltd. Later, in 1963,

Courtesy Ted Gosling

Courtesy Ted Gosling

it was owned by South Devon Cinemas. Like many cinemas of the 1930s, it ran a Saturday morning programme for children. The site is now occupied by the Windsor Gardens. Prior to the opening of the Regal, films had been shown, on a part-time basis, at the Town Hall, which still stands close to the site of the old Regal. I am indebted to Mr Ted Gosling for photographs, both of the cinema and its later demolition. [27.10.97]

The sad end of yet another movie house, as the Seaton Regal is demolished. The area is now a pleasant park

Sidmouth Cinemas: 1924 - 1935

The Grand   High Street   1929 - c1950   FE   F / D

The Grand was not the first purveyor of cinema culture in Sidmouth. Prior to the opening of the Grand, films had been shown first in the Manor Hall and later in the Drill Hall. It seems that the first films to be shown were at the Manor Hall around 1910. This venue, along with the Drill Hall, was almost certainly a part- time venture, though whether on a regular basis I have been unable to discover. The Grand had an imposing façade, with three large windows on the first floor. Steps led up from High Street to the entrance doors in the centre of the façade, and a glass canopy ran the full width of the façade. This, together with the foyer area, survived the fire that destroyed the rest of the building circa 1958. Sadly, this canopy has now gone too. When I spoke with the owner of the restaurant that now occupies the old foyer area, he explained that the wooded frame of the canopy reached a stage of decay that made it a danger to the public and so had to be removed. [22.6.98]

Courtesy J. Clare

The Grand, Sidmouth, showing Olivier's Henry V.

Author's collection

The Grand, Sidmouth, as it now appears, minus canopy.

The Radway Theatre & Cinema, Sidmouth, a rather unusual façade, now one of Peter Hoare's cinemas.

The Radway Cinema & Theatre: detail of façade.

The Radway Cinema   Radway Place   c1930 - present   CWC

The Radway Theatre & Cinema, to give it its full name, has had several owners over the years. The 1935 edition of KD gives the owners, unlikely as it seems, as 'Sidmouth Motor Co & Dagworth Ltd.' By 1939 the same publication lists the owner as Charles F. Cheshire. The 1969 KYB gives the proprietors as Miles Jervis Cinemas, King's Cinema, West Bromwich, Staffs. At that point the cinema had seating for 390, making it a typical small town cinema; compare the Palace at Crediton with 365 seats. Prices in 1969 were 4/6d and 5/6d. By 1976 the seating has risen to 399. Currently, the Radway is one of four cinemas run in Devon by Mr Peter Hoare. Viewed from across the road, the cinema seems bigger than the seating numbers would suggest. When I saw the Radway [22.6.98], it was looking rather neglected. Several windows in the rear of the building were broken and it was certainly in need of a coat of paint. I was not able on that occasion to view the interior. With cinema attendances rising quite rapidly at present, and given the increased profits this rise should bring, there is every reason to hope that cinema owners will again be able to afford to spend more on the maintenance of their cinemas. Buildings of this age and size must present major problems to their owners in terms of upkeep costs. The comments above are not in any way intended as a criticism of individual owners, they merely reflect the difficult times through which cinema has gone in the past fifty years. It is greatly to the credit of cinema owners, especially those owners of single venues or small circuits, that they have continued to provide us with big screen entertainment throughout those lean years, and we should all be grateful to them for the service that they have provided. [22.6.98]

South Molton Cinemas: 1924 - 1935

The Savoy   New Road   1932 - c1950s   BE

When I visited this ex-cinema in 1997, I was amazed at the state of preservation, both without and within. The reason soon became apparent when I discovered that the father of the present occupier, Mr John Fleming, had been a cinema manager in the 1930s. The love of cinema runs in the family. Mr Fleming was so kind as to lend me his father's album, containing photographs and cuttings from the 1930s, when Mr Fleming Snr. was

The Savoy, South Molton, one of two cinemas built by Mr. G. Eastmond, the other being the Plaza at Braunton

manager of the Burlington cinema in Torquay. The exterior of the Savoy, South Molton, is as built, and although the interior is now used as an auction room, it too has preserved much of its former charm. The Savoy was in fact built by Mr G. Eastmond of Tiverton, who also built the Tivoli cinema in Tiverton. This was a typical small-town cinema reflecting, however indirectly, the then current style of cinema architecture, somewhere between Art-Deco and the functional style imported from the continent. I would guess the seating capacity to have been approximately 350 to 400. Adding to the particular interest and excitement of this cinema is the fact that the projection room is still there with all its equipment. [18.7.97]

The auditorium of the Savoy, beautifully preserved. The present lessee is Mr John Fleming, whose father was manager of the Burlington in Torquay in the 1930s.

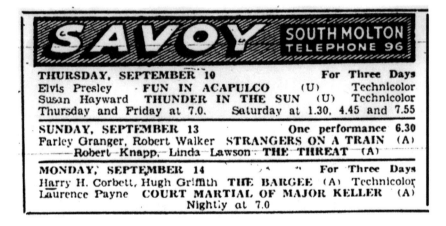

SAVOY SOUTH MOLTON
TELEPHONE 96

THURSDAY, SEPTEMBER 10   For Three Days
Elvis Presley   · FUN IN ACAPULCO   (U)   Technicolor
Susan Hayward   THUNDER IN THE SUN   (U)   Technicolor
Thursday and Friday at 7.0.   Saturday at 1.30, 4.45 and 7.55

SUNDAY, SEPTEMBER 13   One performance 6.30
Farley Granger, Robert Walker   STRANGERS ON A TRAIN   (A)
Robert Knapp, Linda Lawson   THE THREAT   (A)

MONDAY, SEPTEMBER 14   For Three Days
Harry H. Corbett, Hugh Griffith   THE BARGEE   (A)   Technicolor
Laurence Payne   COURT MARTIAL OF MAJOR KELLER   (A)
Nightly at 7.0

Tavistock Cinemas: 1924 - 1935

The Carlton   Plymouth Road c1935 - c1970   BE

The Carlton was owned by E.J. & W.E Pope, who also owned the Carlton cinema in Okehampton and one in Liskeard. It was built in the 'castellated' style to fit in with other public buildings in the town, which had been erected by the Bedford family when the town was still prospering from the profits of copper mining. Mr Pope's son, who still runs the Carlton in Okehampton, spoke of this cinema as his favourite of the three cinemas owned by his father. This may have been because he lived in the town and this was where he got his early

The Carlton at Okehampton, one of very few cinemas still in private hands. Used in Ron Bendell's television documentary celebration Century.

Mr John Pope in the Carlton projection box, see text.

training in cinema management and projection skills. Mr Pope tells me that by the time he was 12 he could run an entire programme on his own. He still enjoys running the cinema and never looks on it as work, though he is tied to the cinema six nights a week.

The Carlton in Tavistock has a place in the history of the area other than as a purveyor of Hollywood dreams. At the height of the Plymouth blitz, thousands of Plymothians were leaving the city each night and heading out into the surrounding countryside. On the 30th of April 1941, many more 'refugees' arrived in Tavistock than had been anticipated, and the cinema was opened up as an additional rest centre. Further information on this aspect of the war in Devon can in found in Gerald Wasley's excellent book on the Plymouth bombing entitled *Blitz*. The exterior of the building can still be seen, looking very much as it did when open as a cinema. [21.9.96]

Teignmouth Cinemas : 1924 - 1935

Winter Garden / Carlton   Carlton Place   c1932 - 1950s   F. D

The Carlton was up and running by 1935, when the proprietor was A.R. Phern, who also owned the Lyceum in Somerset Place, Teignmouth, and the Scala, Dawlish at this time. He continued to own these cinemas up to the start of the Second World War. All three cinemas had ceased operation by the end of the 1960s. I have been unable to find out any real details of this cinema, which closed after a fire in the 1950s and was subsequently demolished. In 1940 the seating is given as 350, making it quite a small cinema. The seat prices at that time were in line with other cinemas in the area ranging from 9d to 1/6d [1996]S

Tiverton Cinemas: 1924 - 1935

Tivoli   23 Fore Street   1934 - present   CWC

The Tivoli was the second cinema to be opened in Tiverton, the Tiverton Electric Theatre having opened in the town in 1911. In 1934 Mr Gregory Eastmond decided that the town would benefit from a second picture house. When I spoke to him in 1997 he was in his 93rd year but still full of plans and ideas for the future. He described how he came to build the Tivoli:

Author's collection

I was at the Empire Leicester Square with the lovely Lorna, with no money in my pocket, and we saw Broadway Melody [1929] and I thought 'Well now' .. ..I was so thrilled with the film, so absolutely thrilled, I dumped my beautiful Lorna in London and came back to Tiverton and built the Tivoli and the one at South Molton [The Savoy]. I couldn't tell you how much it cost to build, all I know is, that in total I hadn't got 6d in my pocket. But my father guaranteed the account at Lloyds Bank so we could borrow the money and build the theatre.....It took about 40 weeks to build and the builder was Mr Grater. I can't remember when South Molton closed. ... The Tivoli ? ...My sons run it now. [T 7.10.97]

The Tivoli was designed by the architect Gerald Saunders, who was also responsible for designing a house for Mr Eastmond in the Art-Deco style. The design for the house was to be seen at the Royal Albert Museum's Spring 1998 exhibition, along with a current photograph of the cinema. Mr Mike Jackson currently leases the cinema from the Eastmond family. I visited the Tivoli on the 1st November 1996 and I spoke to Mr Jackson, who had then been running the cinema since May 1996. I asked Mr Jackson why he had gone into the

Courtesy Mr Francis Eastmond

Francis Eastmond's schoolboys' diary, entry recording the fire at his father's cinema in 1956.

Author's collection

Foyer of the Tivoli, a cosy cinema that still welcomes its patrons and looks on them as friends.

exhibition side of cinema, having previously been a projectionist and film editor. His reply was very illuminating:

Life's ambition. Life's ambition since I was kid. When I was a little tiny tot I spent all my time in the local cinema, turning round watching the beam more than the screen. I used to ask if I could go in the projection room. That was just magic up there. When I left school in 1962 I saw an advert. in the local paper saying the Odeon in Peterborough wanted a trainee projectionist. It was like a gift from above. I got the job and was there for 6 years. [T. 1.11.96]

A picture taken at the opening of the Tivoli in December 1932.

Courtesy Mr Francis Eastmond

The Tivoli, like the Gaumont in Exeter, is set back from the road and is approached by a tunnel-like entrance. The cinema is a single storey building with the seating originally all on one level, but after a fire in the 1950s this was altered to stadium seating. The projectors currently working in the Tivoli came from the Electric Theatre in Newport Street when that closed. I asked Mr Jackson to give me some idea of current (1997) running costs of a cinema of this size, a 400 seater: '*Rent is now £100 a month, rates £250 a month and film transport is about £100. We like to average out at 45% per show to cover costs and that's going some in a place like this. You get peaks and troughs.*' [T.1.11.96]

The Tivoli is a very pleasant, friendly cinema which still has a the right atmosphere to encourage cinema-going as a habit. [1.11.96]

Topsham Cinemas: 1924 ~ 1935

Matthews Hall Cinema / Rex   Fore Street 1928 - 1936/7 - ??   BE

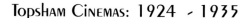

Author's collection

Topsham. Matthews Hall Cinema, first run by Major Gould.

The information that I have on this cinema, along with that relating to the Cosy Cinema in Topsham came from the late Mr Lionel Gould, whose father, Major Henry Charles Gould, ran both these cinemas in the 1920s and 1930s. As stated elsewhere, Major Gould was something of a 'renaissance man' with many and varied interests. With the building of the Matthews Hall, Major Gould removed his cinema shows to this new venue, which was designed with this use in mind. It is still possible to see the projection ports in the rear wall of the building. Boddy & Dempster were the architects and the builder was H Gould & Sons. The building is constructed in brick and has a certain 1930s look to it. The hall is still in use, though it is no longer used for the showing of films. The first talkie shown at the Matthew Hall was *Palmy Days*

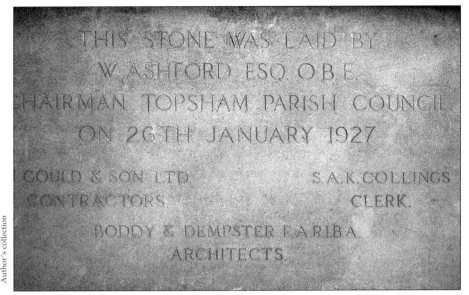

Topsham, Matthews Hall Cinema, built by Major Gould.

(1932) starring Eddie Cantor. Films continued to be shown here by Major Gould until 1936/7. By 1939 Mr A.G. Curtis is given as the proprietor. Mr Lionel Gould had many memories of his family's involvement in cinema exhibition, which he shared with me on my visits to his home in Topsham. The one that seemed to amuse him most was the story of how *Frankenstein* came to be shown in Topsham. It was Lionel Gould who got wind of the refusal of Exeter magistrates to grant it a licence to be shown in Exeter. He telephoned his father with the news and so:

When Exeter banned the showing of Frankenstein, my father, Major Gould, after some reluctance, booked the film to be shown in Topsham on the following Monday. First it had to be seen and approved by the local magistrates. They left this till the Saturday morning. Sir James Owen, chairman of the magistrates, gave the 'go ahead' and the film ran to packed houses all the next week. [T.2.5.96]

I have been unable, so far, to find a final closing date for this part-time cinema. There is no mention of this venue in the KYB 1963, which would suggest that it closed in the 1950s. [2.5.96]

Tudor Cinema, St. Marychurch, Torquay.

Tudor Cinema   Fore Street: St. Marychurch 1926 - c1970s   BE

This was a small, privately-owned cinema that stood in Fore Street, St. Marychurch and is now a museum known as 'Bygones' which specialises in 'Victoriana'. The cinema was still running in 1969 but had closed by 1976. In 1969 the KYB gives the seating as 480 and the proprietors as the Tudor Theatre (Torquay) Ltd with Mr F.L.M. Ellis as the managing director. Performances were nightly with a Saturday matinée. The façade, in mock Tudor, suggests that this may have been a purpose-built cinema, but it is equally possible that we are looking at the conversion of existing premises. It is suggested that The Tudor was able to carry on, long after many other cinemas had closed, due to its situation out of the main centre of population with a locally loyal clientele. Usually it was the smaller cinemas that had to close because dwindling audience numbers made such venues uneconomic. Only the large circuits were able to continue, with the larger profitable venues helping to support the smaller, less economic venues. And even in the larger venues it was often the sales from the foyer kiosks that kept them afloat. I noted on a recent visit that the cinema ticket machine was still in situ. [13.6.2000]

Odeon (ex-Theatre Royal)   29, Abbey Road 1933 -   CWC*

The Odeon Cinema, Torquay, began life as the Theatre Royal in 1863. Accounts suggest that it was never a very profitable operation, despite a great deal of enthusiasm and hard work on the part of its owners. A full account of the theatre can be read in E.N. Stevens' & R.S.Casley's *The Theatre, Abbey Road, Torquay 1863 - 1933*. A so-called cinema lantern was installed in the theatre in 1915. After this date, the programme at the Theatre Royal included films and variety as well as the more usual drama. In 1922 a cinematograph licence for twelve months was initially granted to the proprietors. At the 1932 A.G.M. of the Theatre Royal, an offer of £20,000 was made by W.C. & E.J Vickery, who offered to take on a 21 year lease to run the building as a full-time cinema. This was in addition to four other cinemas that they already managed in the county. The vote was 18 to 4 in favour of accepting this offer. The last live show at the theatre took place in November 1931. The building was re-modelled, the architects being Healy & Overbury of Cheltenham. One source says that when the theatre became a cinema in 1933, both the screen and the balcony were reversed.

Author's collection

Copycat audience. These were a very popular series of postcards that reflected current attitudes to the movies.

Odeon Torquay, former Theatre Royal, an imposing façade with much interior detail worth studying.

Author's collection

In 1933 the old Theatre Royal re-opened as the Royal Cinema with W.G. & E.J Vickery as the proprietors. The opening ceremony was conducted by the Deputy Mayor, Councillor d'Espinsey. By 1939, the Royal had become part of the Oscar Deutsch empire and re-named the Odeon, which it remained till 1999. It was being twinned in 1976/7, by which time, of course, it had long been a Rank Theatre. I visited the cinema in 1996, when I met the manager Mr Stewart and was fortunate in being given a guided tour of the building by Mr Ray Houlton, the senior projectionist. The façade is in the classical style which, in my opinion, is marred by the neon Odeon sign attached to the two pairs of cental pillars; neither does the canopy, which stretches the whole length of the façade, do anything to improve matters. However, given a little imagination, one can still see, behind the modern clutter, the theatre as it once was. The interior is much as one might expect of a building with such a long history. Hidden away behind the screen of Screen 1 is the old proscenium arch of the earlier theatre. Downstairs is the site of the old dressing rooms and on the walls here can still be seen some original gas fittings. A place of ghosts! However, the projection room puts all such fancies to flight with the gleam of state-of the-art projection equipment. This is a cinema that still speaks of the days of Clark Gable, Greta Garbo and long queues in the rain on dark winter evenings. There is now talk of a multi-screen complex for Torquay and, if this comes to fruition, there must be some doubt regarding the future of the Odeon, ex-Theatre Royal. [6.6.96] In fact, since the above was written, the Odeon in Torquay - along with the Drake in Plymouth, and the Torbay Picture House in Paignton - closed in the Autumn of 1999. The Torquay ex-Odeon then re-opened as the Central on February 11th 2000. The present owners have plans, so I was told by the assistant manager Mr Matt Warner, to increase the screens from two to five. [13.6.2000]

Odeon Torquay: a gas-light fitting in the old dressing room area.

The Regal / ABC   Castle Circus   1933 - c1971   D

The Regal, Torquay's second purpose-built cinema, opened in July 1933. It was owned by the same company that ran the Burlington in Union Street. Later the Regal became part of the ABC circuit. In the 1969 edition of the KYB the seating capacity is given as 1499: given the competition from so many other forms

Torquay Regal, now only the name remains.

of entertainment now available, this was really an uneconomic number. The Regal, along with so many other cinemas, suffered from falling attendances from the late 1940s onwards. Audiences fell dramatically after the peak years of cinema attendance in the mid 1940s. Many cinemas were converted to bingo halls and some to supermarkets. This brought the wheel full circle, as many cinemas in the early years of the century were opened in converted skating rinks when the skating craze died out. (There had been a national roller skating craze which reached its peak around 1910 but then rapidly fell away.) The Regal, I believe, was one of those venues that turned to bingo in the hope of staying afloat. This did not work and, after standing empty for a while, the building was demolished in 1989. [1996] S

Totnes, Royal Seven Stars, an early venue for movies.

Totnes Picturedrome

Doors open 7-40 p.m.
Commence 8-0. sharp.

Proprietor—JAMES CLYMO.
Manager—CECIL POPE.

= Programme =

FRIDAY and SATURDAY, DEC. 19th and 20th.

1.—A Knife of Fire
Interest

2—Poor little Chap
Comic

3—The Gangsters
Comic

4—Pathe Animated Gazette

5—His Magic Hand
Comic

Interval of 10 minutes

6—MARY STUART
Drama   (3 parts)

GOD SAVE THE KING.

☞ This Programme is subject to Alteration

Pictures changed each Monday and Thursday.

Totnes, Picturedrome: a typical early programme.

TOTNES CINEMAS: 1924 - 1935

Seven Stars Assembly Rooms   **Mill Lane, The Plains**
1925 - c1928   **BE**

This was a cinema that was running as part of an hotel. In fact, it was the second such venture in Totnes: the Seymour Hotel, where the cinema was known as the Prince of Wales Theatre, had previously had a licence to show films. The 'cinema' in the Seven Stars, I have been told, was in the Assembly Rooms of the hotel with an entrance in Mill Lane. When I spoke with one of the management team of the Seven Stars, in 1997, they were unable to give me any information on this venture. However, the Totnes Museum gave me access to their archives and I am indebted to them for much of the following information. In 1925 application was made, by a Mr L. James, for a licence to run a cinema in the Assembly Rooms of the Seven Stars. This request was granted and Mr H.G. Tapley was appointed as manager. The cinema opened on the 14th March 1925. This venture seems to have run for three years until 1928. A new venture by Mr Tapley brought this short-lived venture to a close. [1.8.96]

The Totnes Cinema   **27 Fore Street   1928 - 1944**   **F**

This cinema, built by Mr Tapley, replaced the cinema at the Seven Stars. It was built on the site of the old Post Office and opened by the Mayor on 22nd December 1928. The cinema was said to be fire-proof, being of iron and concrete construction. The cinema was built and decorated by the Totnes firm of W.J. Goodridge & Son. The interior is described thus: a foyer with auditorium behind, decorated in blue and gold, with some living accommodation above. It was intended to be not just a cinema, but a multi-use building for concerts, meetings etc. A stage and dressing rooms were included in the design. The first film shown was *The Rookies,* with Karl Dane and George K. Arthur [*The Rookies,* MGM 1927 - black & white silent]. The

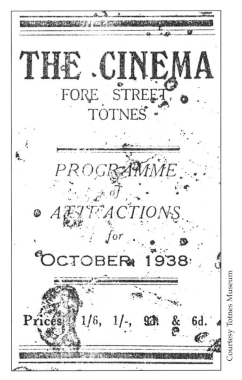

THE CINEMA
FORE STREET,
TOTNES

PROGRAMME
of
ATTRACTIONS
for
OCTOBER 1938

Prices   1/6, 1/-, 9d & 6d.

Totnes, Programme of The Cinema 1938.

prices were as follows: 2/- balcony, 1/3d stalls and 9d & 6d pit stalls. It was here, in 1931, that Totnes cinema-goers had their first experience of the 'talkies'. The first sound film to be shown was *The Dark Red Roses*. [Dark Red Roses - British Sound Films using Phonofilm. Trade showing in October 1929.] The Phonofilm sound system was invented by Dr Lee De Forest, previously mentioned in connection with his invention of the audion tube. The use of this system, first demonstrated in Britain in 1923 at the Finsbury Park Cinema, for a series of British 'talkies' was announced but the producing studio burnt down in October 1919.

Fire, ever a hazard in the world of moving pictures, was responsible for the demise of the Totnes Cinema. Fire broke out in the early hours of March 4th 1944, and the cinema and its equipment were totally destroyed. It would appear that all Mr Tapley was able to save from the blaze was his parrot. The loss of the cinema, at a time of constant 'House Full' notices, was a real blow, the more so since there were hundreds of US servicemen in the area at that

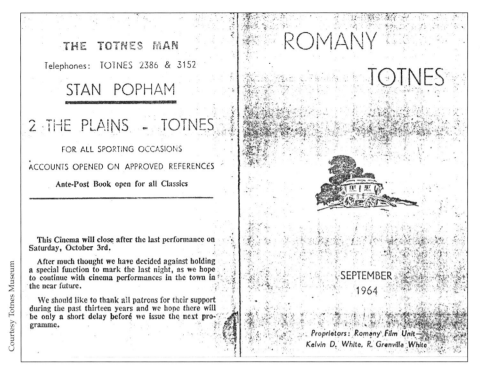

THE TOTNES MAN

Telephones: TOTNES 2386 & 3152

STAN POPHAM

2 THE PLAINS - TOTNES

FOR ALL SPORTING OCCASIONS

ACCOUNTS OPENED ON APPROVED REFERENCES

Ante-Post Book open for all Classics

This Cinema will close after the last performance on Saturday, October 3rd.

After much thought we have decided against holding a special function to mark the last night, as we hope to continue with cinema performances in the town in the near future.

We should like to thank all patrons for their support during the past thirteen years and we hope there will be only a short delay before we issue the next programme.

ROMANY

TOTNES

SEPTEMBER
1964

Proprietors: Romany Film Unit
Kelvin D. White, R. Grenville White

Totnes, closing programme of the Romany 1964.

time, all anxious for their share of Hollywood escapism. [1996]S

Another Totnes Cinema, which needs more research is the Central / Romany. A programme for September 1964 states that 'the cinema will close after the last performance on Saturday October 3rd.' From the same source it appears that this venue opened in 1951. It was owned by 'The Romany Film Unit' - K.D. & R. G. White. The cinema ran in a hall in the rear of what is now the Harberton Art Workshop.

DEVON CINEMAS
1936 - 1939

This brief period was an important one in the history of cinema. It was the last period, until the coming of the Multiplex, in which there was a major cinema-building programme. With the coming of the Second World War, all cinema building came to a halt in this country, as a result of the war-time building restrictions, which also curtailed any repairs to damaged picture houses. The period also saw the final flowering of the Hollywood studio system, of which *Gone with the Wind* is a supreme example. By the time peace was restored to the world, there were many factors which, taken together, caused the demise of the Hollywood studio system which supplied eight out of ten films that the public saw at their local cinema, whether in the splendour of the big town Odeon or in the more humble local picture palace. The Justice Department of United States government had long been trying to break down the stranglehold that the eight main studios had on the distribution and exhibition of films: the decision, in the Paramount case, to force studios to sell off their cinema chains, effectively broke this stranglehold. At the same time, Olivia de Havilland won her case against Warner Brothers over the standard seven year studio contract. While all this is a long way from Devon, it was to affect all cinema-going from the late 1940s onward. Those who can remember going to the cinema in the thirties and forties can look back on a 'golden age'. Never again would cinemas be so luxurious and never again would the patrons be made to feel so important, with the brightly-uniformed staff of the local Gaumont or Odeon seeing to their every need.

Author's collection

'Golden Age' of cinema. 1934 Annual.

Some interesting films on release between 1936 and 1939:

N.B.: Unless otherwise stated, all films from this point on are sound films.

1936	*Triumph of the Will*	*Leni Riefenstahl*	*Documentary*
1936	*Mr Deeds Goes to Town (US)*	*Frank Capra (d)*	*Gary Cooper: Jean Arthur*
1936	*Fury (US)*	*Fritz Lang (d)*	*Spencer Tracey Sylvia Sidney*
1936	*Rembrandt (UK)*	*Alexander Korda (d)*	*Charles Laughton Elsa Lanchester*
1936	*Night Mail (UK)*	*John Grierson (d)*	*Documentary*
1937	*Dead End (US)*	*William Wyler (d)*	*Sylvia Sidney Joel McCrea*
1937	*Le Grande Illusion (Fr)*	*Jean Renoir (d)*	*Jean Gabin Eric von Stroheim*

Courtesy Bill Douglas Centre cn: 3447

A Capra classic. Film tie-ins are not new.

Snow White, the most popular and long-lasting of all the animated films: the first film I saw, aged four.

1937	A Star is Born (US)	William A. Wellman (d)	Janet Gaynor Frederic March
1937	Snow White & the Seven Dwarfs (US)	Walt Disney	Disney's first feature length animation
1938	La Bete Humaine (Fr)	Jean Renoir (d)	Jean Gabin Simone Simon
1938	Pygmalion(UK)	Anthony Asquith (d)	Leslie Howard Wendy Hiller
1939	Gone With the Wind (US)	Victor Fleming (d)	Clark Gable Vivien Leigh
1939	The Stars look Down (UK)	Carol Reed (d)	M. Redgrave Margaret Lockwood

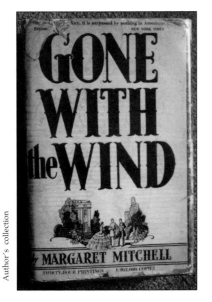

Gone With The Wind, the Hollywood studio film to beat all Hollywood studio films. It still works today.

Fan magazines of the 1930s. We all kept up to date on films and stars with these and similar film magazines.

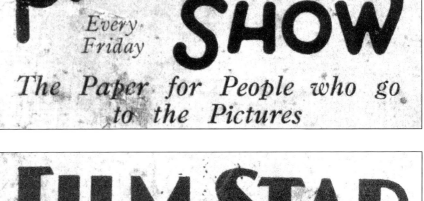

Barnstaple Cinemas 1936 - 1939

Regal   **The Strand 1937- c1980**   **BE**

The Regal still stands in the Strand though it is no longer a cinema. The exterior is little changed since it opened in 1937. It now has had the rather doubtful privilege of appearing in an exhibition, mounted in 1998, of Devon Eyesores. This has nothing to do with the structure as such, but for the way the

Courtesy Denis Knight

Courtesy Barnstaple Records Office

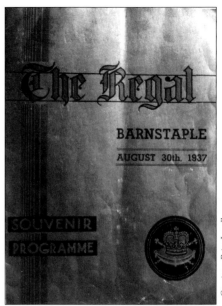

Courtesy Peter Jewell

exterior was then painted. An architect's drawing of the proposed Regal appeared in The North Devon Journal at this period. The caption with the sketch tells us: *Sketch drawn by Mr B.M.Orphoot, A.R.I.B.A., of the new Regal Cinema about to be erected on a site in the Strand at Barnstaple, opposite the municipal Bus Station. The new cinema will supersede the present Albert Hall Cinema...The new Regal house, in addition to 'the last word' in cinema comfort and equipment will be equipped with a full stage and dressing-room accommodation for the production of stage plays. The Architects are Messrs Orphoot and Whiting, A.R.I.B.A.*

The Regal opened on Monday 30th August 1937. The opening ceremony was conducted by His Worship the Mayor of Barnstaple, Captain S.W. Slatter. There was only the one performance that day, at '7.30 pm precisely.' The Regal still appeared in the FTVYB in 1976, when the seating was given as 845, with continuous performances. The manager was Mr. F.G. Yeo. [17.7.97]

Bideford Cinemas 1936 - 1939

The Strand   Kingsley Road   1939 - c198   D

The Strand must have been the last cinema to have been built in Devon before war-time building restrictions put a stop to all such enterprises. The State, St. Budeaux, is also in the running for this doubtful honour It was a simple, almost utilitarian, structure, brick built throughout, and one that was sorely missed when it was demolished. The Strand, with formal gardens and trees around it, must have had one of the prettiest settings of any cinema in Devon. The 1969 KYB gives the seating capacity as 816, making it a fairly typical medium-sized picture house of the period; by 1975 this figure had fallen to 798.

Courtesy Peter Christie

The Strand Bideford, an excellent study.

Photographs taken during the war years show the Strand and, in the foreground, a collection of army vehicles including DUKWs. The caption to this photograph, which appears in *The Book of Bideford*, states that the town's anti-aircraft guns were mounted on the roof of the cinema. One wonders what the noise factor was like during an air-raid, but presumably the cinema was evacuated in such an event. The cinema was demolished in the 1980s. [16.7.97]S

DEVONPORT CINEMAS 1936 - 1939

The Forum today, a very well cared for exterior, even if it no longer draws us to an evening of cinema magic.

Forum   **Fore Street   1938 - 1961**   **BE**

The Forum was the last of the many cinemas to be built, which had provided Devonport with its share of Hollywood films. It was also one of the very few to survive the severe bombing of Devonport in the early 1940s. Given Devonport's crucial importance to the Royal Navy during the Second World War, it is not surprising that it suffered so badly at the hands of the Luftwaffe. It speaks volumes for the modern steel and concrete construction of the Forum that it stood four square when all around it older buildings were reduced to rubble. Contemporary photographs taken soon after the blitz on the night of 23 April 1941, which appear in the Evening Herald publication *Plymouth at War*, show the Forum suffering from what appears to be superficial blast damage. The façade is pock-marked, glass has gone from all the windows and part of the canopy has been torn away; only the letters FORU still remain. Despite the damage caused by this raid, the Forum continued in operation throughout the war years; it was still operating as a cinema when falling audience numbers did, in 1961, what the Luftwaffe failed to do in 1941- i.e. caused the closure of the Forum Cinema. The building is still there and looking much as it did when opened in 1938, but such was the appalling damage caused by the blitz of Devonport that it is impossible to visualise the area around it. [16.4.97]

Forum. Devonport Pre Blitz c1939

EXETER CINEMAS 1936 - 1939

The damaged Forum Devonport (right of picture); the cinema continued to function, I'm told.

Savoy / ABC   **London Inn Square   1936 - 1956 - 1987**   **D**

The first evidence that I possess of the Savoy, later (1956) to be known as the ABC, is a photograph of the Plaza cinema with, in the foreground, the foundations of the Savoy being laid. A much later set of photographs (1987) show the demolition of the same building. Yet another intermediate photograph (taken during the Second Word War) shows the Savoy standing, slightly damaged but proudly defiant, amid the rubble of the blitz. This could be the story of many of Devon's cinemas during this period. Of the 14 cinemas mentioned in this section, 8 have since been demolished - none due to war damage, however.

Photographs of the Savoy taken over the years, often show the much-loved Theatre Royal in the background. An early picture of the Savoy shows just this scene, with the Gary Cooper classic *Mr Deeds Goes to Town* (1936) showing at the Savoy, with Reginald Porter-Brown at the Compton Organ. The blitz picture, circa 1942, has already been mentioned. A later photograph shows the ABC / Savoy (both names appear on the façade at this point) decorated for the Queen's Coronation. The film being shown was *The Man in the Iron Mask* (1939), a strange film to have chosen at such a time, one would think. In the background, the Theatre Royal, similarly flag-bedecked, is advertising *Worms Eye View*. Unfortunately it is not possible, from the photograph, to say whether this was a stage presentation or the film version (1951). In 1969 the KYB gives the seating as 1816, with continuous performances. A later photograph, with the letters E.M.I. covering the former Savoy logo, sees the cinema as a combined cinema / bingo venue. The films on show, *Sweeney 2* and *Saturday Night Fever* would suggest 1978 as the year. The last of this series of photographs shows workmen dismantling the E.M.I. neons on the façade: where the films would have been advertised on the front of the canopy are the words: 'Bye Bye Exeter and Thanks 1936 - 1987'. I have a further set of colour photographs, taken by Mr Dick Passmore who also supplied the first picture, showing the construction of the Savoy, detailing the actual demolition in 1987. Thus the story comes full circle in just fifty years. [1996] S

The Savoy decorated for the Coronation, 1953.

The Odeon, Exeter: Architect's drawing from the opening programme (Robert Bullivant) 1937.

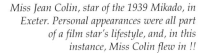

Exeter Odeon: opening programme, details.

Odeon   Sidwell Street   1937 -   CWC

The Exeter Odeon, designed for the Harry Weedon firm by Robert Bullivant, who designed the majority of Oscar Deutsch's empire, had a grand opening on 30th August 1937. The opening was performed by A.C.Reed Esq., J.P, C.C., M.P. This was preceded by the National Anthem and followed by a Musical Interlude by the Band of the 4th / 5th Royal Dragoon Guards. A collection was taken in aid of the Royal Devon & Exeter Hospital. The main feature was *Charge of the Light Brigade* starring Errol Flynn and Olivia de Havilland, supported by *British Movietone News, The Old Mill Pond (Coloured Cartoon)* and *Blonde Bomber*. This was an all 'U' programme. The proprietors are given in the opening programme as Odeon (Exeter) Ltd. and the Resident Manager was Mr. J.A.N. Reid. The main building contractor was P.W. Wilkins and Son, Torquay. The opening programme is couched in the usual 'modest' language of the day. I quote as follows from the introduction:

The coming of the ODEON is an epoch in the entertainment life of Exeter. It is a distinct and unique addition to the amenities of the town, and those who have pioneered in the past must regard it as a compliment that their enterprise has made this theatre possible. The most advanced principles of theatre-cinema construction have been embodied in the design, and patrons will find that in all the 2,000 seats, no matter where they sit, perfection of reproduction will be enjoyed in absolute comfort.... The Staff of specially trained usherettes and attendants will be at your disposal..their primary considerations being courtesy, efficiency and willing service to patrons.

Miss Jean Colin, star of the 1939 Mikado, in Exeter. Personal appearances were all part of a film star's lifestyle, and, in this instance, Miss Colin flew in !!

Written under a portrait of Mrs Oscar Deutsch, the same programme has this to say:

The charming and capable wife of our Managing Director, who takes a very active part in the design and arrangement of all artistic matters in connection with ODEON theatres. Mrs. Deutsch, in co-operation with the Construction Department, is responsible for the selection of colours and the design of the interior decorations and has so far accomplished the remarkable achievement of producing an original scheme for each Theatre, no two theatres on the whole ODEON circuit being similar.

One of Harry Clare's eye-catching adverts 1939.

The programme, as was normal practice at the time, gives a complete list of contractors who worked on the project, from steel work to seating, from vacuum cleaning plants to uniforms. At the bottom of a page showing future attractions and a cut-out slip to request 'your free monthly programme', was a brief note that says it all : 'GET THE ODEON HABIT.'

Odeon, Exeter. Manager Harry Clare, with a lot of happy children, circa 1939.

As mentioned in the section on the Newton Abbot Odeon, I was lent the scrap-book of Mr Harry Clare, who was manager of the Exeter Odeon in the late 1930s and into the war years. This scrap-book is a gold mine of social, as well as cinema history. The following letter to Harry Clare from Oscar Deutsch, dated 14th December 1940 tells a great deal about the times, and the spirit in which people went about doing the job as best they could under those trau-matic conditions.

Dear Clare,

It is with great pleasure that I send you the 'Kinematograph' weekly Plaque for your fine efforts in keeping the flag of ODEON flying with some memo-rable publicity during the past year. I first of all want to congratulate you on your energy and showmanship and as a token of my personal appreciation of your efforts, I want you to accept the cheque enclosed herewith. I deplore the fact that this year I am unable to present this to you in person owing to the unhappy conditions existing, but you may rest assured that because of these very conditions under which you have carried on the good work, I am doubly appreciative.

Yours sincerely,

O. Deutsch

The 'unhappy conditions' referred to in that letter are spelled out in a photo-graph showing Harry Clare in the auditorium of the Odeon, surrounded by a sea of school children all holding up their gas-masks. Another photograph shows a 1937 Hillman, masks on the head lights, bonnet draped with a Union Jack, and the whole surmounted with a stuffed lion's head advertising the Korda film *The Lion Has Wings*. A cutting dated 7th April 1941, together with a picture of the happy couple, tells of the wedding of cinema usherette Miss M.M. Moore to a member of the Royal Air Force. The film on show was *Quiet Wedding*. I rather suspect the hand of Mr Clare in the timing of this event; the informal reception was held at the cinema, as the bride's friends from the cinema were unable to attend the wedding owing to a morning matinée. One

This was an advertisement that surely caught the mood of that moment in history.

other item from this period is worth recalling. It made both local and national press and resulted in yet another letter of appreciation from Mr Deutsch. To help patrons leaving the Odeon in the blackout, Mr Clare had the cinema commissionaire's cap and uniform outlined in luminous paint. Sadly, these personal letters from Oscar Deutsch were soon to be a thing of the past. Oscar Deutsch died on 5th December 1941 at the early age of 48. In such a short time he had built up an entertainment empire of which any man might be proud. He wrote the following in the journal *Design and Construction* in March 1937, and it might well serve as a very appropriate epitaph:

It was always my ambition to have buildings which were individual and striking, but which were always objects of architectural beauty..we endeavoured to make our build-ings express the fact that they are specially erected as the homes of the latest, most progressive entertainment in the world today.

Cathedrals of the Movies - David Atwell -Architectural Press -1980   [1996+]

Hope Cove Cinemas

The Barn   **The Square   c1938 - c1946**   **D**

In the same period in which the Odeon in Exeter was amazing its patrons with all that was 'brightest and best' in the world of cinema going, other venues also had their loyal patrons, and not all of them were on the same scale or offered the same luxury. However, if I am honest, of all the cinemas, ex-cinemas and sites that once held a cinema, that I have visited in the past four and a half years, it is the Barn at Hope Cove that holds pride of place in my affections. This cinema, a former part-time venue, was brought to my attention by the following letter from Mr R.C.S Raine of Cambridge:

Dear Mr Chapman,
*   Although not a cinema, films were certainly shown to the public in Inner Hope, Hope Cove in 1939. In a barn at the top end of Inner Hope 'square' there were numerous Disney Cartoon characters painted / drawn on the walls of a stone and cob barn. I looked for it a few years ago but reality didn't match my memories of those times...'*

The Barn cinema in Hope Cove September 1938.

The Barn, Hope Cove: Marcia leads the way.

This letter was dated October 8th 1996. This was followed two days later by a similar letter from Mrs Janet Loder of Bideford, who had also spent childhood holidays in the Thurlestone area and remembered the Hope Cove cinema. I followed up these letters by a visit to Hope Cove on the 18th of October in the same year, when a Mr J. D. Sleightholme told me that the barn had been demolished and bungalows now stood on the site. This site is at a point where the path to Bolt Tail leaves the village. Mr Sleightholme later sent me a photograph of the Barn Cinema in operation. I made no further progress with this site until a Devonshire Association member put me in touch with Mr John Jarvis of Hope Cove. When I visited Mr Jarvis on 7th May 1998, he shared with me his memories of going to the Barn cinema:

'I went there, yes. Used to see... spiders come down across the screen, off the thatched roof, ... spiders in the middle of the film...'

Mr Jarvis was also able to sketch the building as it had been in those days. He then put me in touch with Mr Dudley Stidson, whose father owned the barn when it was a part-time cinema. Mr Stidson kindly saw me that same day and talked to me about the time, the late thirties and forties, when his family ran the Barn Cinema. He also showed me cuttings and photographs from the family album relating to the Barn Cinema.

There's my father on horseback with the cattle [photograph showing the Barn Cinema]. *There's my sister, Marcia, taking the money from the people... It was owned by my father W.R. Stidson. .. We had a chap called Jack Merrington at Hope Barton Farm and he was very keen on cinema, so they decided to create a cinema in this old barn.* [It was a thatched building] *They managed to get some seats out of an old cinema somewhere in Devon, and luckily the inside of the building, it was oblong, it had a sloping floor. They put all these old bucket seats, the red ones, in this building, and where they had the screen it was surrounded with all the old crab pots and fishing nets. ...But the most interesting part about it is that the fishermen of Hope Cove, a lot of them had never been outside the village in their life. They were fishermen and this particular man Jack Argeat, and he was 85 I think, he had never been to a cinema in his life and he didn't understand what it was. We invited Jack Argeat to come to the cinema this particular night and the film was* Turn of the Tide [starring Geraldine Fitzgerald and Wilfrid Lawson]. *It was about a typical fishing village, like Hope Cove, where the fisherman all went out to sea, fishing and crabbing. There was a terrible storm... We invited him to see the film and he just sat there in wonderment. An old man, wonderful it was, fantastic.* [T: 7.5.98]

Marcia takes the movies to the villages -1946

One photograph in the album was clipped from the Daily Express; the original snap had been sent by a holiday visitor to the Daily Express as an entry in a 'Holiday Snaps Competition'. A similar photograph was from the local Evening Herald: the latter is dated Tuesday 20th September 1938. Mr Dudley Stidson's elder sister Marcia was married to Mr. Dick Holman who, with Jack Merrington, actually ran the cinema. Marcia was taught to use the projector and when her husband joined the forces, Marcia carried on showing films, not only in Hope Cove but also touring the villages. A photograph in the album shows Marcia with her projector in Yealmpton. Mr Stidson thought that this was taken about 1946.

I have written at length on this particular part-time cinema for two reasons. Firstly, although more and more research is being undertaken and published with regard to the urban super-cinemas, these tiny rural venues are in danger of being lost forever. It was only a happy chance that put me on its track. Secondly, the story of the Barn Cinema is a timely reminder of just how rural many parts of England still were, as late as the start of the Second World War. [18.10.96]

Ivybridge Cinemas

Cinedrome   **Fore Street   c1938 - c1950s**   **D**

This is another small, semi-rural venue which has been demolished and about which I have been unable to find any real details. When I spoke in December 1996 to Mr Hawken, who had been a projectionist at Ivybridge, he was far from enthusiastic about the Ivybridge cinema. He said it was: *"The worst cinema ever. There was no water, no toilets and no heating. .. The projection box broke all fire regulations.... It was always wet and dripped. The cinema was in an old mill. ... The power was DC ... went down to the sub-station to turn off some village power to allow the cinema to work on Mondays and Thursdays."* Mr Hawken then moved on to work in the Gaumont, Plymouth, which Mr Hawken states had the same projectors as the Cinedrome, Ivybridge. Mrs Rosemary Paul, who now lives in Cawsands, grew up in Ivybridge and remembers attending the cinema there. It was, Mrs Paul remembers, much used by the USAAF personnel billeted in the area during the Second World War. Mrs Paul tells me that a Mrs Strutt delivered the films to the cinema. The building was demolished during redevelopment and I have been unable either to trace pictures of the building or to locate its actual site.

Newton Abbot: Harry Clare liked using cars, it seems.

Courtesy John Clare

Odeon   Wolbrooke Street   1936 - c1970s   D

I had despaired of ever finding any illustration of this cinema, when I had the good fortune to be approached by Mr John Clare whose father, Mr H.H.(Harry) Clare was manager of the Odeon, Newton Abbot in the mid thirties. Mr Harry Clare had kept an album of photographs and cuttings from the time when he worked as manager of the Odeon in Newton Abbot and later the Odeon in Exeter. Mr John Clare kindly loaned me the album and allowed me to make any copies that I felt would be useful to this research. From the album it is possible to build up a picture of the daily life of a cinema and its staff from the mid thirties to the mid nineteen forties.

The Odeon, Newton Abbot, was actually built by the Paignton Picture Company, Mr J.J. Mann tells me, and then sold to the Odeon Circuit. Among the papers in the album are several letters signed by Oscar Deutsch. One such was a letter congratulating Mr Clare for winning the local area exploitation competition. The letter ran as follows:

Newton Abbot Odeon:
a very professional advert.

Dear Clare,

Exploitation Competition - January.
It is with great pleasure that I enclose herewith a cheque for £3 .3. 0., being the First Prize in your area in the above Competition. I must congratulate you upon your splendid exploitation, and, at the same time, tell you how pleased I am with the efforts made by your brother Managers throughout the Organisation.
Your achievement in winning the First Prize is all the greater because of the excellent entries that have been submitted. The judging of this Competition has been very difficult, and I have found it necessary to increase the number of Second Prizes to fifty, instead of five. I sincerely hope that your success in the first Monthly Competition will spur you to even greater efforts, and I shall look forward to your future entries with great interest.

Yours sincerely,

O. Deutsch

This letter is dated 18th February 1938. In order to save space, I have omitted the paragraphing in the original. Mr Clare was to receive other such letters from Oscar Deutsch, including one in December 1940, by which time he was manager of the Odeon, Exeter. In those far off and gentler days, a film did not get the multi-million dollar publicity of the 1998 film *Titanic;* managers were expected to and indeed did create their own publicity. A photograph from this same album shows a Morris Ten with loud-speaker on the roof, together with a wooden jungle cut-out advertising Dorothy Lamour in *Hurricane*. Attached to the front bumper is another cut-out bearing the slogan: 'At The ODEON Newton Abbot'. Mr Clare tells me that his father did all this type of advertising himself, using his fretwork set. A night photograph of the Newton Abbot Odeon at the time of George VI's Coronation shows the façade surmounted by a huge, cut-out imperial crown, covered in metallic paper. Running along the front of the canopy were the words : GOD BLESS THEIR MAJESTIES. The film showing at this time was Charles Laughton in *Rembrandt,* which was followed later in the week by Will Hay in *Good Morning Boys.*

The Odeon, Newton Abbot,
decorated for the 1937 coronation.

Unfortunately, the 1969 KYB gives no details for the Odeon, Newton Abbot. By the time of the 1975/6 edition of the FTVYB, the cinema had closed. [1996]S

Carlton　　　　St. James Place 1938 - present　　　　CWC

The Carlton was one of three cinemas owned and run by Mr W.E. Pope, the father of the present owner, Mr John Pope. When I spoke to Mr John Pope early in 1998 he had this to say about the building of the Carlton Cinema:

"Before the cinema was built, the site was occupied by a cluster of very small slum houses. It was I think, though this was before my time, like two rows of very small cottages with a courtyard in the middle with three wells. ....which must have been filled in ....We've never had any problems with them since. The construction is concrete block. The roof is supported merely on girders, so you could knock the walls out and the roof would still be there. This was deliberately done because, you know, nobody knew if the cinemas were there to stay. So the roof is totally independent of the walls. They are like steel arches that hold the roof up and the ceiling battens are bolted to them as well. The heating had originally been a coke boiler, then oil and then gas. The original chimney was a large pipe, which rusted and had to be replaced. There used to be two rear exits, though now there is only one. Originally it seated about 600." [T.9.3.98]

I find it interesting that at so late a date as 1938, a cinema builder had serious doubts about the financial viability of setting up a new cinema. However, it should be borne in mind that Okehampton was not a large town and that the surrounding population was small and scattered. Mr Pope makes the point that nowadays, with greater individual mobility and better roads, the film-goer is able to travel to Exeter or Plymouth to see the latest block buster in the 'first run' houses.

Courtesy Tom Endacott

Carlton, Okehampton: buying the site.

The Carlton, Okehampton: the rather austere façade.

Author's collection

In about 1953 Cinemascope was installed. This meant bringing the screen forward about 15 feet with some loss of seating. The seating today is for 350. When I asked Mr Pope how audiences today compared with those in the heyday of cinema in the thirties and forties, when cinema was a habit, he had this to say:

"It depends on the film, and that's the be all and end all of it. Its got to be a film that they want to see. I think the regulars today are the 14 to 20 year olds, and because they've got to see the film immediately it comes out, they're all off to Exeter, so you don't get them a lot. So basically here it's family films and those like the present Titanic. If you put on something that's aimed exclusively at the teenage audience its not much good, they've probably already been to see it in Exeter, which is now only

20 minutes away where as it used to be three quarters of an hour."
[I commented that there was no car park for the cinema.]

"I don't think that's a great problem, nobody moans about it, Luckily the street is quite handy and we soon fill it up. Nobody says we don't come because of the parking."
[I then asked Mr Pope whether a block buster like Titanic affected admissions.]

"Yes but probably admission-wise Babe, the pig picture, did as well, but on money terms, purely because it's adults and not children, Titanic is way ahead of it. That's the reality of it."

Mr Pope, commenting on the present strip lighting, had this to say:

"The lights were originally five fairly large round lights in a metal frame.... quoting from memory, with individual triangular glass pieces in them. They were round and inside were ordinary bulbs and the glass was just painted colours. But the bulbs used to go so often and they were difficult to get at. But we had bingo here in the 1960s, just one night a week, and the strip lights were put in so that they could see.

On Coronation Day 1953, if there was rain in the afternoon, you had to put on a film that was suitable for children which anybody could go to for nothing. But it didn't rain and I remember my father was quite delighted."

Author's collection

The Carlton, Okehampton: original fire hose

Mr Pope does all the projection himself, which means that he is working six nights a week, throughout the year. When I asked if he still enjoyed running a cinema, I got the following answer, which is remarkably similar to the one given by Mr Mike Jackson who runs the Tivoli in Tiverton:

"Oh yes. I don't look on it as work. I was interested in it as a youngster. My parents never forced me into it. We lived at Tavistock, at Spring Hill and when I was 11 or 12 I used to go down there [The Carlton in Tavistock was also owned by his father] *quite a bit, but they didn't push me into it and they didn't tell me to keep away. I gravitated up to the projection room and I was shown how to do things. By the time I was twelve I could put a show through on my own. I used to enjoy it and it's something that gets into the blood. You speak to other people who do it, run cinemas, like the chap at Bude and they're all ex-projectionists or it's been in the family and they all enjoy it. I don't look on it as work."* [T 9.3.98]

There is much in what Mr John Pope has to say here that seems to hark back to the way of life of the fairground families, who were, after all, the pioneers of cinema in this country; a way of life that is almost extinct. The coming of the multi-plex and the 'fast food' attitude to be found in many cinemas today, strongly suggests that cinema-going is entering, has perhaps already entered, a new and very different mode. Whether, even with increasing attendances, this new mode will generate the former love of cinema is far from certain. However, some things remain constant. The 1909 Act, though now some ninety years old, still plays a part in the life of the cinema owner. The safety of the patron is still the main concern of the authorities.

"We had this obnoxious fire officer [though this was many years ago, it is still vivid in Mr Pope's memory] *and he really ripped the inside out of it. It was the time all the softboard in the ceiling had to be painted with fire retardant paint, the exit had to be blocked on the outside* [I assume this to be the one at the rear of the building that was made redundant when the screen was moved forward in the 1950s] *and numerous other little things, you know, and he really just frightened me to death. This one really picked on it and of course it all had to be done within the year, which it was. But ever since then, I view a fire inspection with a little bit of trepidation, purely because of that experience. No, we don't get a lot of problems really. I always imagine it to be far worse than it actually is. I tend to worry about it, it's on your mind a bit, because whatever you do they don't bother to look at, there's always something you've forgotten to do that they see. I always think, what else is there I can do?"* [T. 9.3.98]

I have quoted at length from this interview with Mr John Pope because the Carlton, being typical of many of Devon's market town cinemas, surely reflects much of their history too. [9.3.98]

Paignton Cinemas: 1936 - 1939

Odeon (ex-Palladium)   Abbey Road 1939 - c1950s   D

The story of this cinema has already been covered in a former section under its original name. I include it here as yet another example of a local cinema becoming part of one of the large national circuits. The Odeon circuit under Oscar Deutsch, was one of the most distinctive and successful of these circuits. It was only the early death of Oscar Deutsch in 1941 that saw this circuit absorbed into the Rank Empire.

Plymouth Cinemas: 1936 - 1939

State / Mayflower   Victoria Street, St Budeaux   1939 - 1960s - 1973
BE

I visited this ex-cinema in 1997 and was impressed by its stately, if now rather shabby exterior. The construction is in brick, now bearing the name boards for both a carpet sale room and the Victoria Snooker Centre. The building has a solid and somewhat uninspiring look. Rust has begun to affect down pipes and it is difficult to imagine it in its former glory, though there was little glory in its early years. The cinema opened on 16th November 1939, soon after the start of the Second World War. This must be the last pre-war cinema to have been built and opened in Plymouth before war-time building restrictions came into force. The first film to be shown was *That Certain Age* [1938] starring Deanna Durbin, then at the height of her fame. (In 1938 she was awarded a Special Academy Award for 'bringing to the screen the spirit and personification of youth'.) The cinema had seating for 750 patrons with prices ranging from 6d to 1/- The cinema, unlike so many others in Plymouth, survived the blitz. In the 1969 edition of the KYB the seating is given as 935, with seat prices given as 3/6d to 4/6d. The owners are Gwent and West of England Circuit Ltd (Cardiff). At about this time, the name was changed to Mayflower and the

The State, St Budeaux, en fête for a film festival.

cinema soon became part of the Rank Circuit. The cinema turned from films to bingo and by the time of the 1975/6 edition of the FTVYB, the cinema had disappeared from its pages. [25.6.97]

Royal/ABC/MGM/ABC   Derrys Cross   1938 - present   CWC

The Royal, which suffered many changes of name in more recent years, was opened in 1938. It was built on the site of the old Theatre Royal, which had been demolished in 1937. This old theatre, built c1812, had been gutted by fire in 1878 but was restored in that same year. The new cinema was built to the design of William Glenn and still stands proudly at Derrys Cross, having been almost isolated in a sea of ruin by the blitz. It opened on 15th July 1938 and the ceremony was conducted by the Lord Mayor, Alderman S. Stephens J.P. The cinema boasted a Compton Organ, played at the opening by Wilfred Southworth. Prices at this time were 6d, 1/-, 1/3d and 1/6d. Having survived the war years, the cinema has also survived the changing pattern of

The Royal, now to become the next Odeon, I believe.

The Royal/ABC/MGM etc, a very typical cinema building of the inter-war years, which replaced the old Theatre Royal.

attendances. This survival depended on various strategies at different periods. The KYB 1969 gives the seating as 2,124, a huge number considering that audiences declined annually from the late forties until the mid eighties. In 1954 the cinema introduced live theatre as part of the programme to combat the decline, a reversal of the pattern of earlier days when cinema was brought into theatres to combat falling theatre attendances. Later, wide screen was fitted to encourage people back into the cinema. In 1958 the cinema officially became the ABC. But with audiences still on the decline, other measures were needed if the cinema was to survive. In 1977 the cinema was remodelled and now has three screens, Screen 1 seating 583, Screen 2, 380 and Screen 3, 115. This represents a loss of some 1000+ seats, but it was an effective move as the cinema is still functioning, when many other large cinemas throughout the country have been forced to close. With a new multiplex now open in Plymouth (Warner Village) the future of the ABC is once again in the balance. It would be a tragedy if Plymouth's one remaining pre-war cinema was forced to close its doors at a time when cinema audiences are again on the increase. [16.1.97]

Courtesy Rosie Oxenham

The Town Hall Cinema, Princetown: part of the BB Cinema circuit run by Major J.H.Blackhurst.

PRINCETOWN CINEMAS: 1936 -1939

BB Cinema / Town Hall   Town Hall   c1939 - 1989   D

Princetown never boasted a purpose-built cinema, but films were shown here, at the Town Hall, on a regular basis. It was a typical multi-use building and it was demolished in December 1989. The cinema appears in KYB 1939 under the name of the B.B. Cinema, with J.H. Blackhurst as the proprietor. As it does not appear in the 1935 edition of KYB, I am assuming that it opened between 1935 and 1939. I have been unable to discover when the last film was shown here. I am also assuming that this was a part-time cinema, given the size and isolated position of the town. Later research revealed that the BB Cinema Circuit was owned and operated by Captain J.H. Blackhurst, whose headquarters were in Cross Park, Bickington. The BB Cinema Circuit, which ran part-time programmes, operated in 1935 in the following locations, each shown in KYB 1935 as a BB Cinema:- Lynton, Hartland, Morchard Bishop, South Molton, Dulverton, Princetown and Gunnislake. A similar, though much smaller operation, was run by Mr Street from Torpoint in Cornwall. Mr Street served three venues at that time, in Callington, Millbrook and Ivybridge, with two shows weekly.

The demolition of the Town hall, an event that was totally ignored, I'm told, by both ex-patrons and the press.

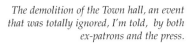

Courtesy Rosie Oxenham

DEVON CINEMAS
1940 - 1945

This period, together with the last year of the previous section, covers the entire span of the Second World War and saw no cinema building in this county. The one exception, the State cinema in St. Budeaux, was so near to completion in 1939 that building was allowed to continue, and the cinema opened in December 1939. In 1939 it is estimated that there were about 5,500 cinemas nationally; by 1946 this figure had dropped to 4,714. The story of these years is one of cinemas lost to enemy action (in Plymouth, Devonport and Exeter) and of ever-increasing audiences, culminating in the peak year of 1946. In that year there were approximately 1,635 million cinema admissions or 31 million tickets sold each week in this country. These are national figures but the same pattern would be reflected here in Devon. As in the Great War, civilians and servicemen and women turned to the cinema to seek warmth, comfort and a couple of hours of escape from the horrors or boredom of war. In this war, the civilian was in the front line in a way that had not been true of the earlier conflict. This was a period in which the British film came to the fore. The documentary tradition that had grown up here during the thirties, with such brilliant directors as John Grierson, now came to full flower. This tradition not only produced some superb documentaries, such as *Fires Were Started*, but its influence can also be seen in many feature films of which Noël Coward's *In Which We Serve* is a prime example.

It was amid scenes like this that the cinema played its most important role. But all too often those cinemas became part of the rubble. This is Exeter: similar scenes were just as much a part of life for the people of Plymouth or Devonport.

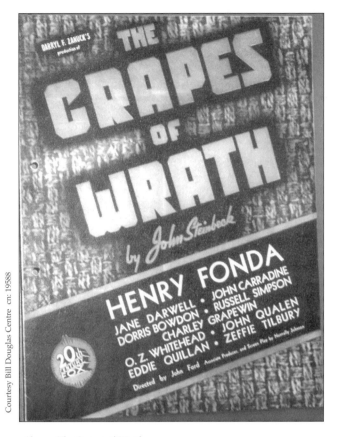

*Above: The Grapes of Wrath,
John Ford's hard-hitting film
with a documentary
feel to it; one of his best.*

*Above right: Orson Welles'
Citizen Kane still tops many
lists of top ten films:
his first biography.*

Some Important Films On Release 1940 - 1945

Title	Director	Starring
The Grapes of Wrath (1940)	John Ford (US)	Henry Fonda
		Jane Darwell
Citizen Kane (1941)	Orson Welles (US)	Orson Welles
		Joseph Cotten
Target for Tonight (1941)	Harry Watt (UK)	CFU*: Documentary
		Service cast
Next of Kin (1942)	Thorold Dickinson (UK)	W.O.Documentary
Millions Like Us (1943)	Launder & Gilliat (UK)	Eric Portman
		Lili Palmer
Fires Were Started (1943)	Humphrey Jennings (UK)	CFU : Documentary
Ox-Bow Incident (1943)	William Wellman (UK)	Henry Fonda:
		Dana Andrews
Henry V (1944)	Laurence Olivier (UK)	Laurence Olivier
		Robert Newton
Les Enfants du Paradis (1944)	Marcel Carné (Fr)	Arlette: Jean-Louis
		Barrault
Western Approaches (1944)	Pat Jackson (UK)	CFU: Documentary
Brief Encounter (1945)	David Lean (UK)	Celia Johnson
		Trevor Howard

[* CFU = Crown Film Unit]

Far left: This was one of the finest of the documentary films produced in Britain during these difficult years. Tragically, by the end of the war most the aircrew of F Fred were dead.

Left: Les Enfants du Paradis, made during the occupation, is a brilliant film, one to watch again and again.

Cinemas Lost 1940 - 1945

Included in the following list will be some 'ex-cinemas' which had ceased to show films prior to the Second World War but which might still be extant as buildings, had they not been destroyed at this time. The date when they ceased to function as cinemas will be shown in square brackets by each such cinema. Cinemas that suffered some damage but continued to function are shown in ( ) brackets.

The Palladium, Ebrington Street, Plymouth

Plymouth Cinemas Lost 1940 - 1955

Cinedrome	57 Ebrington Street	1941	Façade remains extant
Criterion	13/14 Cornwall Street	1941	Became Weaver to Wearer [1938]
Embassy	193 Union Street	1941	Formerly Gaiety / Carlton
Grand Theatre	Union Street	1941	Former theatre turned cinema
Lyric	34 Union Street	1941	Became Lyric Dance Hall [1916]
Palladium	27 Ebrington Street	1941	
Savoy	108 Union Street	1941	Formerly St. James Picture Hall

The Grand, Plymouth: interior awaiting demolition.

Devonport Cinemas Lost: 1940 - 1945

Electric	Fore Street	23rd April 1941	
(Hippodrome)	Princes Street	April 1941	Damaged, never reopened as cinema [1939]
Tivoli	8 Fore Street	23rd April 1941	
(Forum)	Fore Street	23rd April 1941	Damaged, but continued to function as a cinema

The Hippodrome, Devonport. Majestic in defeat.

Courtesy Tony Moss

Exeter Cinemas Lost: 1940 - 1945

Empire Electric	248 High Street	1942	[1937] Owned by the Devon & Somerset Stores.
Lounge	9 Fore Street	1942	[1937] Formerly the City Palace.
Palladium	93/94 Paris Street	1942	[1938?] Formerly Queen's Hall.
Plaza	London Inn Square	1942	Formerly the Hippodrome.
(Gaumont)	11/12 North Street	1942	Damaged, but continued to function as a cinema.
(Savoy)	London Inn Square	1942	Damaged, but continued to function as a cinema, following closure and repairs.

The Palladium, Paris Street, Exeter.

Exmouth Cinemas

Savoy   Rolle Street   1940s   Bomb fell on cinema during
                                         performance: didn't explode.

This means that, in the period 1940 to 1945, ten full-time cinemas were lost in the three towns of Plymouth, Devonport and Exeter, at a time when audience numbers were increasing almost weekly, reaching their peak in 1946. As we shall see in the next section, this loss rate was minuscule when compared to later closures due to falling audiences.

DEVON CINEMAS
1946 - 1995

'Theatres and cinemas are also assets to a centre such as Plymouth and seriously affect its position as a resort; and while not so urgently necessary as the re-establishment of housing and commerce, they must be provided if the city is to regain its former attractiveness. The serious depletion of the city's accommodation in this particular branch of entertainment will be realised when it is stated that no less than 10 out of 19 buildings have been destroyed or rendered useless.'

> A Plan for Plymouth 1943 - The Report prepared for the City Council by J. Paton Watson, City Engineer and Surveyor, and Patrick Abercrombie, Consultant.

This span of fifty years was to see a long period of decline in cinema attendances, with the resulting closure of large numbers of cinemas. This decline did not show any signs of easing until 1984; since that year there has been a slow, but steady increase in cinema attendances, and this upward trend has accelerated during the latter part of the 1990s. Blockbuster films such as the previously-mentioned *Titanic* have played their part in this cinema renaissance, together with the introduction into this country, from America, of the multiplex cinema. Before considering the implications of this upward trend, we need to go back and see just how falling numbers actually affected cinemas. Numbers tell the story in very plain terms: in Devon in 1939 there were at least 75 full-time cinemas in 39 towns. By 1945, taking into account the 10 lost in the blitz, Devon was left with 65 cinemas. However, by 1969 there were only 32 cinemas left in 22 towns, showing that, since 1939, at least 17 towns were now without a cinema. The picture gets worse, for by 1976 there were only 26 cinemas in 15 towns. Between 1969 and 1976 the following towns lost their only cinema: Braunton, Crediton, Cullompton, Honiton, Kingsbridge, Seaton, Tavistock and Great Torrington. Plymouth had only four cinemas; Newton Abbot was reduced to one cinema (the Alexandra) although Torquay at this time still boasted three cinemas. At a later stage, Kingsbridge, Tavistock and Great Torrington were to initiate part-time cinemas. In 1995, when I began the research on which this book is based, the number of cinemas in Devon had fallen to 13 full-time cinemas in 12 towns, as listed below:

Plymouth:	MGM (ABC) and Drake Odeon
Exeter:	Odeon
Torquay:	Odeon (ex-Theatre Royal)
Newton Abbot:	Alexandra
Barnstaple:	Astor (ex-Gaumont)
Okehampton:	Carlton
Ilfracombe:	Pendle Stairway Cinema

DEVON CINEMAS

1947

* Cinema

Ilfracombe * *

Lynton *

Braunton *

* Appledore

Barnstaple * *

Bideford * *

Gt. Torrington *

South Molton *

Holsworthy *

Tiverton * *

Okehampton * *

Cullompton *

Crediton *

Honiton *

Chagford *

Moreton'h *

Tavistock * *

EXETER * * *

Ottery St. Mary *

Topsham *

Bovey *

Axminster

Princetown

Ashburton *

Sidmouth * *

Seaton *

Buckfastleigh *

Budleigh *

Exmouth * * * *

Newton Abbot * * *

Dawlish *

Devonport * *

Teignmouth * *

Plympton

Plymouth
* * * * * *

Ivybridge

Totnes *

Torquay * * * * * *

Paignton * * * *

Brixham *

Kingsbridge *

Dartmouth *

Salcombe
* *

N.B. These figures are taken from KYB 1947

Gordon Chapman: January 1999

Sidmouth:	Radway
Teignmouth:	Riviera
Exmouth:	Savoy
Tiverton:	Tivoli
Paignton:	Torbay Picture House

Of these, only one is a post war cinema, The Drake, Plymouth. However, there have been many changes in the past two years, with cinemas closing as the multiplex makes its presence felt. The Picture House in Exeter, a small two-screen cinema which opened in recent years, is currently a successful venture in the city. As I write (June 2000), the Warner Village complex has opened in Plymouth, and the , Apollo multiplex in Paignton (a conversion of the Festival Theatre). It is also encouraging to note the opening, though on a much smaller scale, of the Reel Cinema in Kingsbridge, which took place in May 2000. This replaced a part-time cinema on the same site. Of similar interest is the story, carried by The Express and Echo [25.6.98], of projected plans for a multiplex cinema and night club, in Exeter, on the site of the present bus station. No further details have been forthcoming at the time of writing.

Picture House, Exeter, taken in August 1998.

The Apollo Cinema, Paignton.
Opened in September 1999,
site of the former Festival Theatre.

Some Important Films on release between 1946 and 1956:

With the exception of the two-screen Exeter Picture House, which opened in Exeter in 1996, the grand opening of the Drake in Plymouth in 1958 saw the end of cinema building in the county until the coming of the multiplex. The Apollo in Paignton and the Warner Village in Plymouth, Devon's first multiplexes, both opened in 1999. The end of cinema- building did not, of course, see an end of cinema- going. However, as the second half of the century progressed, the role of the cinema as an influence on manners and morals decreased. The main audience became the 14 to 26 age bracket. The films they enjoyed were those which reflected their own life style, rather than films to influence that life style. My film list ends at a point, in the mid-1950s, when cinema was losing its hold and influence on the old-style family audience.

Best Years of Our Lives. *Music tie-ins go back to the silent days. Some music is better remembered than the film it was written for, but not in this case.*

Title	Director	Starring
The Best Years of Our Lives, (1946)	William Wyler (US)	Frederic March: Myrna Loy
Great Expectations (1946)	David Lean (UK)	John Mills: Alec Guinness
Monsieur Verdoux (1946/47)	Charles Chaplin (US)	Charles Chaplin: Martha Raye
Louisiana Story (1946/48)	Robert J Flaherty (US)	Documentary
Odd Man Out (1947)	Carol Reed (UK)	James Mason: Kathleen Ryan
Treasure of Sierra Madre (1948)	John Huston (US)	Humphrey Bogart: Walter Huston
Oliver Twist (1947/48)	David Lean (UK)	Robert Newton: Alec Guinness
Hamlet (1948)	Laurence Olivier (UK)	Olivier: Felix Aylmer Basil Sidney
Red Shoes (1948)	Powell & Pressburger (UK)	Moira Shearer: Robert Helpmann
Bicycle Thieves (1949)	Vittorio de Sica (It)	Lamberto Maggiorani, Enzo Staiola
All About Eve (1950)	Joseph L. Mankiewicz (US)	Bette Davis: Garry Merrill.
Sunset Boulevard (1950)	Billy Wilder (US)	Gloria Swanson: William Holden
A Street Car Named Desire (1951)	Elia Kazan (US)	Vivien Leigh: Marlon Brando
High Noon (1952)	Fred Zinnemann (US)	Gary Cooper: Grace Kelly
The Cruel Sea (1953)	Charles Frend (UK)	Jack Hawkins: Donald Sinden

Great Expectations. *I remember seeing this film on its first release, and I still jump back when Magwich leaps out.*

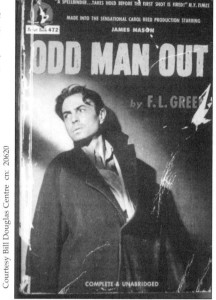

Right: Odd Man Out, perhaps the best film James Mason made , certainly in this country.

Far right: More talked about than enjoyed, one feels, but still brilliant screen Shakespeare.

On the Waterfront (1954)	Elia Kazan (US)	Marlon Brando: Eva Marie Saint
Bad Day at Black Rock (1955)	John Sturges (US)	Spencer Tracy: Dean Jagger
Baby Doll (1956)	Elia Kazan (US)	Karl Malden: Carroll Baker

Plymouth Cinemas: 1946 - 1995

The Drake Odeon   Derrys Cross   1958 -1999

I believe this cinema to be unique in this country as it is the only cinema built by the American Twentieth Century Fox Corporation. However, they soon sold the Drake to the Rank Organisation and it became an Odeon, sited very close to the ex-Gaumont, then Odeon, at 151 Union Street. When I visited the Drake in January 1997, I was fortunate in meeting and interviewing the Senior Projectionist, Mr Ron Wilson. Much of what follows is taken directly from that interview:

> "I started here [The Drake] in May 1958 and we opened here in June 1958 with South Pacific. It was one screen, a 1600 seater. ...It's totally [owned by] Rank. The only reason they [20th Century Fox] built it was that they had made so much money. They had two other shows in London, the Rialto and the Carlton. They made that much money [but] they couldn't take it out of the country so they decided to build the Drake. They kept it for about twenty months. They weren't really interested so they sold out to Rank."

As Ron Wilson says, the cinema was opened on 6th June 1958, by the Lord Mayor of Plymouth, George Wingett. The architect was Leonard Allen F.I.A.A. and builder A.N.Coles. The programme included, besides *South Pacific*, the *'Plymouth Story - a tribute to the people of Plymouth and the building of the city of tomorrow'*. In 1975 the Drake was tripled. Screen 1 seated 919, Screen 2 and 3 seated approximately 168 each. This represents a loss of about 380 seats. However, this was not the end of the story, for in 1991 two more screens were

The Drake Cinema, Plymouth, taken in 1962, showing Union Street and the remains of bomb damage around it.

Courtesy John Slater

added with Screen 1 at 440, Screen 2 at 166, Screen 3 at 166, Screen 4 at 220 and Screen 5 at 120. With the closure of the Odeon (ex-Gaumont) in April 1980, the Drake became the only Odeon in the city and one of only two purpose-built cinemas then still functioning in the city. The days when Plymouth could boast a multitude of picture houses, both great and small, have gone. and so has the experience of cinema-going. Mr Wilson had this to say about the changes:

"Cinemas today are a supermarket compared with your old corner shop. They had time to spend with you, which is how the old cinemas used to be. Now it's like a supermarket, you go in and you have to serve yourself. ...It's a conveyor belt. Get 'em in, let them find their own seats. There's no usherette to show you to your seat. Somebody tears your ticket, gives you back a bit - says: 'you're in row 8 seat 13'. In you go, find your own seat. No sales girls come round with a tray any more. If you

The Drake / Odeon, as it became some two years after it opened. Built by Twentieth Century Fox.

want ice-cream or sweets you walk out to the kiosk and get it. ... I've seen all those days. Where the manager would be there when you went out - "Goodnight, I hope you enjoyed the show". Now you're happy if you see anybody *at the end of the show, let alone open the door and ask if you've had a good evening."*

Mr Wilson illustrated his remarks on the social aspects of cinema in former days with the following true story. It is worth remembering that he is not talking about a tiny cinema in a small market town, but a very large city centre cinema.

"In the old days we had regulars all the time. Pensioners. We used to have one old lady there, all the staff knew her as Gran. She used to live over in Kings Street. She used to come in every day of the week. If we opened at one, she'd come in with her little basket and little flask. It was continuous then. She'd sit in the back stalls downstairs in the second seat...She'd come in at one in the afternoon and go out at ten at night. She had company and it didn't cost her any heating or electricity... She'd come out and say to one of the girls "Would you wind my watch for me?" The girls would

The Senior Projectionist, Ron Wilson, in what had been the Luxury Lounge, then the box for screens 4 & 5.

Author's collection

say "Certainly Gran, have you got everything. Got your flask?" Everybody called her Gran. Lovely old dear she was. ... Bear in mind she's long gone, I'm going back 30, maybe 35 years. [T.17.1.97]

It is obvious from the above that the experience of going to the cinema has changed over the years, and many of us regret these changes. But the experience of cinema-going was never fixed. Many of those who experienced the change from Silents to Talkies felt this same sense of loss while others were delighted by the change. The introduction of colour likewise met with a mixed reception. The first hundred years of cinema has now become part of our cultural and social history. As we move into the second hundred we can look forward to new ways of enjoying 'a night at the pictures.' It will not be the same but there is no reason to doubt that it will be any less exciting.

Chagford Cinemas

Rex   **New Street   c1936 - 1950s**   **BE**

This is another cinema where specific details have not come easily to hand. A telephone call in December 1996 alerted me to its existence, but, apart from the fact that it was closed and now used as a furniture store, no other information was available. It was not until July 1998 that I was able to visit Chagford: the visit proved most useful. The site of the former cinema can be approached either from New Street (where the frontage was) or from a narrow lane leading from High Street past the old boiler house. As I was taking the first of a series of photographs of the building, I was approached by the present owner of the building, Mr John Meredith. Below is a transcript of our recorded conversation:

"I use it for a store. I've got planning permission for it upstairs as a house, but the bottom I use as a store. The actual cinema was on the first floor and you went in through there [black door on the east side of the building]. *The chap who ran it, he rented it and he was very good with his hands, a good craftsman and he made a big REX sign which hung there, all illuminated. I don't know his name, I forget. This is where you went in, we used to queue along here. Then you went up the stairs and there would be a little foyer up there and you paid there."*

The Rex at Chagford, another hidden cinema but safe for the present, and the exterior well cared for.

[Author: You say he had a bathroom behind the screen ?]

"Yes, a bathroom behind the screen. The screen went all the way along there and he had his bathroom in behind there, a little room. The actual flat [in which he lived] *was by the projection room over here* [at other end of building]. *It packed up in the late 50s. TV was coming in and as you know the *** rental of the films, that's what killed it. That's the projection room. He lived at the back here. It looks kind of cin-ema-ry* [sic] *doesn't it ? That's his garden. He had a model railway and it ran all round the wall there. He was very clever with his hands."*

[Author: When did it start, have you any idea?]

"No. Before that it was an Assembly Room. I reckon it started after the war.[In fact it seems to have opened between 1935 and 1940, when it is noted in the KYB 1940, and closed by 1963, for there is no mention in the KYB 1963.] *...had a sign there with all the posters attached. The boiler room* [a small shed-like building in the narrow lane leading to High Street] *was in here with great 4 inch pipes going into it. That's the good seats* [pointing to a section at the rear of the

The Rex showing the all important boiler house. It can be cold on a winter night if you are alone in the flicks.

building over the lane from High Street] *and there were two rows of wooden seats in the front, almost on top of the screen. About 9d I think - terrible eye strain. I've owned the building for 28 years."*

[Author: What happened to all the equipment from the projection room ?]
    "... it all went. The person I bought it from was a builder and he owned it and rented it out to the chap and [he] *just dumped the projectors - arc projectors. It* [the showing of films] *was twice a week Wednesday and Thursday and Friday and Saturday.* [I assume this means that there was a change of programme mid way.] *They didn't do the beginning of the week."*

[Author: What happened to the name board?]
    "I'm afraid I'm guilty of smashing up one. It was a hand- made job. He made it out of tin-plate and he'd fixed a light in it. I took it down. I didn't know the value of anything like that then and it was falling to bits and I took it down because it was going to drop on somebody's head. Pity! Should have kept it."

The front of the building now carries a small, neat sign saying 'The Old Rex Cinema', which I suspect was put there by Mr Meredith. I only wish that all ex-cinemas were clearly marked in this way. The sign is high on the wall above a flight of steps leading down from an old emergency exit.

Author's collection

The Rex, Chagford. The screen end where the owner had his bath, or so I am reliably told by the present owner.

Ilfracombe Cinemas 1946 - 1995

Embassy / Pendle Stairway   High Street   1948 - present   CWC

I visited this cinema in July 1997 and was amazed to discover that it had formerly been both an hotel and a church (Christ Church). As the former, it was first The Great Western and later the Regent Hotel. The Embassy opened on October 11th 1948 and closed on Saturday May 21st 1949. It was reopened, by the Clifton Circuit - which in 1964 was also running the Gaumont, formerly the Scala - on Monday 8th May 1950. In August 1983 the Embassy was bought by Mr & Mrs Tuffin, who in May 1984 renamed the cinema the Pendle Stairway. The cinema is still under their management. The cinema opened in 1948, but the exterior has a very 1930s look. The interior still shows

The Pendle Stairway, Ilfracombe, seen from the street.

Author's collection

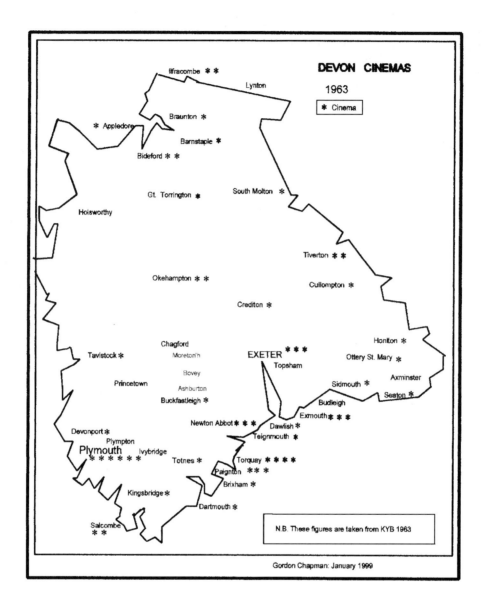

The two main urban areas of the county, Plymouth and Exeter, clearly show the pattern of cinemas closures. The same pattern also occurs in Torquay, one of the main holiday resorts on the South Devon coast. However, these centres still retain some of their picture houses. It is the smaller towns which were the hardest hit by the closures. For example, Chagford, Princetown, Holsworthy and Axminster were without a cinema for the first time in many years. This pattern continued over the following years.

The Pendle Stairway, ceiling to the stairs, very ecclesiastical.

The Pendle Stairway, projection box, heart of any cinema.

physical traces of its former life as a church in some of the internal décor. I was fortunate in being given a guided tour by the projectionist in 1997. A fascinating venue, which shows clearly the way in which a whole range of buildings have been converted into cinemas over the past 100 years.

Part-Time Cinemas

I am including here some part-time cinemas about which I have little information, but which deserve to be included as purveyors of cinema, no less important to their patrons than the large full-time cinemas.

Ashburton Cinemas

The story of cinema in Ashburton resembles that of some other small towns in the county, with the one exception that it never acquired a purpose-built cinema. I am indebted to Mrs Wendy Major for the following account of cinemas, in at least four different venues, in Ashburton. They are not necessarily in chronological order, though Mrs Major felt sure that all were running around the dates given.

The Den (Golden Lion)   c1939 to c1945

This venue, which was the longest running of the Ashburton cinemas, was held at the back of the Golden Lion. Seating about 100, it ran throughout the Second World War when cinema-going was at its height. It was the only one of the four venues to run for any length of time.

London Hotel   1950s

This short-lived venture used the ballroom of the London Hotel, as did the original cinema at the Riviera in Teignmouth.

Ashburton: The Golden Lion, home for a while to a part-time cinema.

The London Hotel, which also hosted the movies.

The site of the Ashburton Picture House, I've been told, but it is very hard to imagine it now.

The Town Hall, Ashburton, which, like so many public buildings, was for time the purveyor of movie magic to Devon's movie fans, both young and old. The Golden Days are gone.

Ashburton Picture House   1950s

This building, now converted to flats, was originally part of the mill complex off Mill Meadow, and was perhaps used for storage. It is now difficult to interpret how the building was used in the days when it showed films. Another Ashburton resident remembers that it was known as the Ashburton Picture House.

Town Hall   1950s

Like so many other towns in Devon, and indeed throughout the country, Ashburton made use of its imposing Town Hall as a part-time cinema. We have seen this pattern in Bovey Tracey and elsewhere.

The Town Hall, Lynton, which was showing films soon after it opened in August 1900. I have seen mention of the showing here, early in the new century, of films by the great French director Georges Méliès. The Town Hall was one of at least three venues in the town. There is even talk of another to come.

Author's collection

Lynton Cinemas

Lynton was 'given' a Town Hall by Sir George Newnes, who performed the opening ceremony on August 15th 1900. A photograph of the occasion appears in John Travis' publication *An Illustrated History of Lynton and Lynmouth.* The photograph shows the Town Hall to be a splendid example of 'mock' Tudor, which would not have looked out of place in many a Hollywood epic set in those far-off days. It appears that, for many years, this was the venue for Lynton's part-time cinema. One source states that film presentations began here as early as the year after the opening ceremony with a Biograph show in September 1901. However, this seems not to have been the only home for cinema in Lynton as a letter I received from Mr Ken Grinstead makes clear:

"You may be interested in my childhood memories of films seen, and buildings used for cinema performances in Lynton in the 1920s and 1930s.

My father took me to see a silent version of The Hound of the Baskervilles, *probably in 1930. I was then seven years old. The film was shown in the upper room of a building in Queen Street. It was south of the Market Hall and opposite Mrs Jeffery's fishmonger shop. It may have been over premises in which a Mr Adams had set up a business making and selling early radio sets. You will be able to find exact information in Directories of the period.*

Later in the 1930s a non-conformist Chapel was converted to a cinema. This building was some 100 yards up Sinai Hill, the old road leading to Lynton Station. Morning shows such as cowboy films were given to the 'lads of the village'. The evening performance was, as I remember, a single show only and I am not sure if there were matinée performances."

Dartington Cinemas

The Barn

It is part of the Dartington Hall complex and runs on a regular, if part-time basis. The design would suggest that it began some time in the 1920s and it has been suggested to me, by the Dartington Hall archivist, that it could possibly have been designed, in part at least, by Walter Gropius.

Tavistock Cinemas

Wharf Centre

When I visited Tavistock in 1996, the Wharf Centre had just re-opened its part-time cinema. It had opened the previous year, but had soon closed. I understand that it is now running on a regular, if part-time basis. This is Tavistock's only cinema since the Carlton Cinema closed some years ago.

DEVON CINEMAS

1976

❋ Cinema

Ilfracombe ❋ ❋

Lynton

Braunton

Appledore

Barnstaple ❋ ❋

Bideford ❋

Gt. Torrington

South Molton ❋

Holsworthy

Tiverton ❋ ❋

Okehampton ❋

Cullompton

Crediton

Honiton

Chagford

Moreton'h

Tavistock

EXETER ❋ ❋

Ottery St. Mary

Topsham

Axminster

Bovey

Sidmouth ❋

Princetown

Ashburton

Seaton

Buckfastleigh

Budleigh

Exmouth ❋ ❋

Newton Abbot ❋

Dawlish

Devonport

Teignmouth ❋

Plympton

Plymouth

Ivybridge

❋ ❋ ❋ ❋

Totnes

Torquay ❋ ❋ ❋

Paignton ❋ ❋

Brixham

Kingsbridge

Dartmouth ❋

Salcombe

N.B. These figures are taken from KYB 1976

Gordon Chapman: January 1999

By 1976 the number of cinemas had dropped below the figure given for 1914. The majoriy of extant ones, including those in Plymouth and Exeter, were still those concentrated in the south of the county. Apart from Okehampton, the centre of the county was devoid of cinemas. In fact, only nine cinemas north of Exeter are shown. However, it is possible that itinerant cinemas brought films to those towns without a full-time cinema, and these would not be included in the KYB figures. When I began researching this book in 1995, there were only fourteen cinemas in the whole of Devon. Some of these would be multi-screen cinemas and therefore would produce an attendance figure in excess of a single-screen cinema. This pattern has accelerated with the introduction of the multiplex cinema such as the Apollo in Paignton and the Warner Village in Plymouth. This gives a wider choice of films to those in the big towns and cities, but offers nothing to the more isolated communities or those without their own transport. Thus, the rural cinema-goer is at a disadvantage, and it is unlikely that this pattern will change.

Conclusion

This book would not have been possible without the unstinting help and encouragement of a large number of people, both those within the cinema business and also members of the public. Their names will be found in the list of acknowledgements. I must also acknowledge the financial help given by the Devonshire Association, who awarded me a small grant to help with the expenses of this project. Others who warrant special mention are: Mr J.J. Mann of the Torbay Cinema, Paignton; Mr Peter Prince of the Riviera Cinema, Teignmouth; Mr Pat Ghillyer CVA and Mr John Baker, both of Plymouth; Mr John Gregory of Crediton; Mr John Pope of the Carlton Cinema, Okehampton; Mrs Anne Elliott of Braunton; Mr Chris Vernon of Ilfracombe. To these and all those who have helped in any way, my grateful and sincere thanks, and my apologies to anyone who has been inadvertently omitted.

Author's collection

The Warner Village, Plymouth, opened 1999 'The Shape of Things to Come'.

I am very aware that, in trying to cover a county the size of Devon and a time span of one hundred years in this research, mistakes may have crept in. Memories fade with time, facts may get muddled as stories are passed down through a family. I have tried, where possible, to get confirmation of information given from at least one other source. However, this has not always been possible, and even written sources do not always agree.

Despite the help acknowledged above, I am solely responsible for the inclusion of any such errors, and would welcome any comments or corrections from readers.

Gordon Chapman: Exeter, July 2000

Selected Bibliography

Atwell, D.,	1980	*Cathedrals of the Movies* (Architectural Press)
Brownlow, K.	1968	*The Parades Gone By* (Secker & Warburg)
Brownlow, K.	1979	*The Pioneers* (William Collins)
Christie, I.	1994	*The Last Machine* (BBC Education)
Drazin, C.	1998	*The Finest Years: British Cinema of the 1940s* (André Deutsch)
Docherty, Morrison & Tracey	1987	*The Last Picture Show?* (BFI Publishing)
Elberts, J. & Ilott, T.	1990	*My Indedecision is Final: The Rise & Fall of Goldcrest Films* (Faber & Faber)
Field, A.	1974	*Picture Palace* (Gentry Books)
Halliwell, L.		*Halliwell's Film Guide* (Grafton Books, 7th edn, 1989)
Halliwell, L.	1985	*Seats in All Parts* (Granada)
Hoskins, W.G.	1960	*Two Thousand Years in Exeter* (James Townsend & Sons)
Houston, P.	1994	*Keepers of the Frame* (BFI Publishing)
Izod, J.	1988	*Hollywood & the Box Office 1895 - 1986* (Macmillan Press)
Kanin, G.	1977	*Hollywood* (Panther Books)
Kracauer, S.	1947	*From Caligari to Hitler* (Princeton University Press)
Low, R. & Manvell, R.	1948	*History of British Film: 1896-1906* (George Allen & Unwin)
Low, R.	1971	*The History of British Film 1918-29* (George Allen & Unwin)
Low, R	1985	*History of the British Film 1929-39* (George Allen & Unwin)

Manvell, R.	1946	*Film* (Pelican Books)
Manvell, R.	1955	*The Film and the Public* (Pelican Books)
Marx, S.	1973	*Mayer & Thalberg* (W.H. Allen)
Mast, G.	1976	*A Short History of the Movies* (Bobbs-Merrill Company)
Norman, B.	1987	*Talking Pictures* (BBC/Hodder & Stoughton)
Park, J.	1990	*British Cinema, The Lights that Failed* (B.T. Batsford Ltd. London)
Perkins, V.F.	1972	*Film as Film* (Penguin)
Perry, G.	1974	*The Great British Picture Show* (Little, Brown)
Puttnam, D.	1997	*The Undeclared War* (Harper Collins)
Rawlence, C.	1990	*The Missing Reel* (Collins)
Robinson, D.	1981	*World Cinema* (Eyre Methuen)
Rotha, P. & Griffith, R.	1967	*The Film Till Now* (Spring Books)
Scrivener, K.	1989	*Plymouth at War* (Archive Publications: *Plymouth Evening Herald*)
Smith, S.	1994	*Cinemas & Theatres of Exeter* (Mercia Cinema Society)
Toulet, E.	1995	*Cinema is 100 Years Old* (Thames & Hudson)
Wenden, D. J.	1974	*The Birth of the Movies* (Macdonald)
Winchester, C. (ed)	1933	*The World Film Encyclopaedia* (Amalgamated Press)
Worrall, G.	1979	*Target Exeter* (Express & Echo)
Yule, A.	1989	*David Puttnam* (Sphere Books Ltd.)

Acknowledgements

The following organisations have given help in various ways during the period of this research:

The Devonshire Association (Branches and Sections); The Devon & Exeter Institution; the Devon Library Service; The West Country Studies Library; Exeter University (Bill Douglas Centre); *The Express & Echo*; *The Evening Herald*; *The Okehampton Times*; *The Crediton County Courier*; *The Western Morning News*; Radio Devon; Axminster Museum; Barnstaple Museum; Ilfracombe Museum; Kingsbridge Museum; Okehampton Museum of Dartmoor Life; North Devon Records Office; Salcombe Museum; Seaton Museum; Totnes Museum; The British Film Institute; The Cinema Theatre Association; The Mercia Cinema Society.

Many people have been very generous with their time and assistance during this project; help from the following individuals is therefore gratefully acknowledged:

Appledore:	Mr & the late Mrs J M Clarkson
Axminster:	Mr Les Berry, Mr Gerald Gosling
Barnstaple:	Mr Peter Jewell
Bideford:	Mr Peter Christie, Mrs Janet Loder
Brixham:	Mrs Cooty
Braunton:	Mrs Dennis, Mrs Anne Elliot, the late Mr Vic Thompson
Buckfastleigh:	Mr R Pickles
Cambridge:	Mr R C R Raine
Chagford:	Mr John Meredith
Crediton:	Miss Carol Furse, Mr John Gregory, Mr A E Labbett
Croydon:	Mr Tony Moss CTA. (President)
County Durham:	Mr Colin Saunders MCS
Cullompton:	Mr D G Williams
Exeter:	Mr Peter Edwards, Mr & Mrs P Jackson, Mr Peter Jarmin, Mr Brian Le Messurier, Mrs H M Ogg, Mr Dick Passmore, Mr G W Radmore, Mrs Sidwell, Mr Michael Tamlyn, Mr Peter Thomas, Mr E Winfield
Exeter:	Image of Empire Cinema by courtesy of the Isca Historical Photographic Collection, Exeter.
Exmouth:	Mr M Rice
Fremington:	Mrs Rosie Oxenham
Hampshire:	Mr Ken Grinstead
Hope Cove:	Mr John Jarvis, Mr J D Sleightholme,

	Mr Dudley Stidson
Ilfracombe:	Mr Chris Vernon
Kingsbridge:	Mr Tim Blyth, Mr T Noyce
Knowle:	Mr John Shanes
Lincolnshire:	Mr Brian Hornsey MCS
London:	Mr Oliver Horsbrugh CTA, Mrs Joyce Taylor
Newton Abbot:	Mr Peter Hoare
Okehampton:	Mr Claude Cockwill, Mr Tom Endacott, Mr John Pope
Ottery St Mary:	Mr Roger Thorne, Mr & Mrs Morris
Paignton:	Mr J J Mann, Mr Robert Letcher
Plymouth:	Mr John Baker, Mr W T Cole, Mr Pat Ghillyer, Mr Peter Hamer, Mr Hawken, Mr Maurice Heath, Mr Colin Heatley, Mrs Olive Milsom, Mr John Milton, Mrs Ivy Northcott, Mrs F G Pack, Mrs Muriel Smith, Mr Ted Southgate, Mr Roy Williams, Mr Ron Wilson, Mr Fred Wiznor, Mrs B Wood
Seaton:	Mr John Clare, Mr Ted Gosling, Messrs. Knight & Staff
South Molton:	Mr John D Fleming
South Zeal:	Mr & Mrs R Radford, Mr & Mrs P Shaw
Starcross:	Mr John Slater
Teignmouth:	Mr & Mrs Peter Prince
Tiverton:	The late Mr G Eastmond, Mr F. Eastmond, Mr Mike Jackson
Topsham:	The late Mr L. Gould
Torquay:	Mr Matt Warner
Totnes:	Mr & Mrs P Flood, Mr Bob Mann, Mr L Irwin
Wiltshire:	Mr David Townsend

My final thanks must be to my wife Maureen and my daughter Fiona, who have not only endured four years of constant 'cinema' talk, but have also typed and proof-read this book in all its many drafts.

Index

An Alphabetical List of Devon Cinemas, Venues and Distributors